FORG
THE KEY TO THE DOOR TO ETERNAL LIFE!

Forgiveness In The Era of Joe Biden, Donald Trump, and Beyond!

Jesus said:

"I am the door: by me if any man enter he shall be saved, and shall go in and out, and find pasture."

- John 10:9.

By:

Franklin D. R. Jackson, Ed. D. →JLPNP←

Copyright © 2022
Franklin D. R. Jackson
All rights reserved.
ISBN: 978-1-959298-85-4

Dedication

I dedicate this book to people of all persuasions -- political, socio-economic, philosophical, ethnicity, gender, religious beliefs, and so forth, who tirelessly and intentionally strive and persist to teach and live forgiveness through their words and deeds. These individuals include parents, siblings, temporal teachers, religious teachers, ministers, and pastors, elected officials, political leaders, governmental officials, and so forth. May you continue to make opportunities to nurture, teach, and practice forgiveness wherever you are. You are the blessed among us.

I want to single out the blessed Reverend, Dr. Martin Luther King, Jr. who was the personification of forgiveness in our time. He taught forgiveness and demonstrated forgiveness as a way of life. I am delighted to dedicate this book to Dr. King and to all of you who strive to forgive and to assist others to do likewise! Blessings and Love to you!

Contents

Dedication 5
Acknowledgments 9
Preface 12
Chapter 1 19
   Introduction
Chapter 2
   Everyone Needs Forgiveness 25
Chapter 3
   Old Testament Models of God's Forgiveness 39
Chapter 4
   Old Testament Examples of Humans' Forgiveness .. 73
Chapter 5
   Jesus Teaches About Forgiveness 92
Chapter 6
   The Greatest Demonstration Of Forgiveness By The God-Man: Jesus! 117
Chapter 7
   The First Act Of Forgiveness Of The Risen Jesus And His Assignment To His Betrayer Peter 128
Chapter 7
   Stephen: A Human Model Of Forgiveness 143
Chapter 8
   The Risen Jesus Forgives Saul 153
Chapter 9
   Paul's Teachings About Forgiveness 162
Chapter 10

Lord, Please, Help Me To Forgive 177
Chapter 11
    Personal Experiences With Forgiveness 191
Chapter 12
    Father, Please Help Me Forgive Him 212
Chapter 13
    The Joy Of Forgiving 216
Chapter 14
    Conclusion 224
Chapter 15
    Epilogue 270
About The Author 287

Acknowledgments

The Old Testament person who I want to acknowledge is Esau. Esau was the first son of Isaac and Rebekah. He was the elder brother of Jacob. By tradition, as the first son, he was entitled to the benefits of birthrights. However, Jacob his younger brother tricked or scamming of his birthright—the right to be the leader of his clan-family and heir to his father and ancestor to Isaac's descendants. Perhaps, even worse than tricking Esau of his birthright, Jacob connived with his mother Rebekah to steal the special blessings Isaac wanted to bestow on his first son Esau. So, Esau vowed to kill Jacob as soon as their father died. Jacob fled from Esau and stayed away for twenty years. Yet when Jacob was returning home, Esau went out and met him. Instead of killing Jacob, Esau ran to meet him, embraced him, fell on his neck, kissed him, and wept. And evidently, Esau forgives Jacob. Undoubtedly, the greatest human forgiveness in the Old Testament. Therefore, I acknowledge Esau posthumously. Esau is certainly the epitome' of human forgiveness in the Old Testament of the Bible.

I turn now to the New Testament of the Bible and acknowledge the greatest demonstration of human forgiveness recorded in the Bible up to that time and perhaps for all times. Deacon Stephen was devoted and outspoken follower of Jesus. Religious leaders were stoning him to death for preaching about Jesus as the Son of God. As Stephen was being stoned to death, he kneeled down and uttered the words of forgiveness, "Lord, lay not this sin to their charge." Such great human forgiveness deserves acknowledgment in a book on forgiveness. So, I am most delighted to humbly acknowledge Deacon Stephen, for his words and deeds of forgiving the seemingly 'hard to forgive.'

Beyond the two biblical characters who I acknowledge, I want to acknowledge my parents, Arnold Scott Jackson, my father and Irine Jackson, my mother, who taught and showed me, from a tender age, the importance of forgiving others. In addition, I am grateful to the numerous secular and religious teachers, ministers, preachers, and others who have touched my life over many years, and have taught and continue to teach the value of forgiveness. I am certainly indebted to them, and acknowledge them. The song writer says,

"What the world needs is love," that is true; however the love must manifest itself in forgiveness. Thanks to all of you who embrace true forgiveness. Please continue to assist others to forgive. Because the world needs more forgiveness. And forgiveness is the key that opens the Door to the Kingdom of God. Blessings and Love to all!

Preface

Target Audiences

I wrote this reader-friendly, easy-to-understand book on forgiveness, primarily for Christians-believers who want to forgive, some of whom are finding it difficult to forgive individuals, such as Former President Donald J. Trump and evangelicals who seem not to understand that forgiveness requires remorse and repentance. The book is also beneficial to some individuals-'Christians' who are finding it difficult to forgive democrats whom some Christians-believers consider as violators of God's commandments and their "First Amendment Rights." In addition, the book will be of tremendous help to not-yet believers who have the desire to forgive and need a little assistance in the forgiveness process.

The book will be helpful to many who are experiencing extreme hurting and excruciating pains. They may include many who lost loved ones through COVID-19 or might be suffering from the impact of the coronavirus. Many of these individuals consider themselves to be Christians-believers, yet they are suffering and are struggling with forgiving others, some of whom they blame for their circumstances.

In addition, the book is for everyday Christians-believers who struggle with the idea or effort to forgive over and over. And who may also be hesitant in seeking God's forgiveness or even embarrassed in seeking God's forgiveness over and over –seventy times seven, as Jesus commanded His disciples to forgive, **"I say not unto thee, Until seven times; but, Until seventy times seven" (Matthew 18:22).** This means to forgive as often as a person genuinely seeks forgiveness.

I once made the astonishing remark to participants in a Bible study class: "It is not because you sin which keeps you from entering the Kingdom of God." And then I paused, and there was stillness-silence in the Bible class. Then I reminded the class of the teaching of Paul, "All have sinned and come short of the Kingdom of God." Then I reminded the class of the Model Prayer, which Jesus taught His disciples, **"And forgive us of trespasses (sins) as we forgive those who trespass against us" (Matthew 6:12).** Luke puts the prayer this way, **"We**

have forgiven those who have trespassed against us" (Luke). Only then did I explain that it is the lack of our ability or unwillingness to forgive others that prevents us from entering the Kingdom of God; because God will not forgive us for our trespasses against Him if we do not forgive those who trespass against us.

So, those of us who claim to be followers of Jesus must try not to be like Jonah—more righteous than God—in deciding who deserves forgiveness and who does not. Similarly, we must not forget that God allowed--enabled Nebuchadnezzar and the Babylonians to destroy Jerusalem and Judah because King Zedekiah—the last king of Judah—refused to humble himself and step down from his throne and surrender to Nebuchadnezzar. He preferred his wives and daughters to be taken by the Babylonians and to see Solomon's Temple destroyed than to humble himself and give up the throne as Jeremiah, the Prophet, beseeched him to do. The analogy is so close between what we are witnessing today and what happened then that I am compelled to write this little book on forgiveness.

I am well aware of the consequences of speaking the truth—Jeremiah was placed in dungeons for prophesying that the Babylonians would capture and destroy Jerusalem. Micaiah was placed in prison when he told King Ahab that he would lose a battle and would be killed even though 400 false prophets told King Ahab what he wanted to hear. In our times, people have lost their jobs, got demoted, endured character assignation, and even been threatened for speaking the truth. I know of a wonderful person who was forced to retire because he dared to raise questions regarding questionable decisions at his place of employment.

So, I am writing this book on the quintessential responsibility of followers of Jesus to be quick to forgive and forget and to encourage evangelicals to be more like Jeremiah and Micaiah and less like the 400 false prophets who told Ahab what he wanted to hear or who told the Jews in captivity in Babylon that they would be back in Judah in a little while—in no time flat. As an ordained evangelist who tries to listen to the Holy Spirit and who sees parallels between Judah of the 640 B. C.—580 B. C. and our times, I am concerned.

I am deeply concerned with the false prophets of our times. Those who purport to represent Jesus must speak the truth—regardless of consequences—or don't speak at all. We cannot be God, but we can be more like God—forgive and forget—even forgiving and forgetting leaders who are unable or unwilling to speak the truth and are deliberately or unknowing bent on hurting the nation and the world.

Prayerfully read this book and ask God to help you to speak the truth, even when it hurts and ask Him to grant you the courage to stand up for the truth and to help you to forgive and forget in Jesus' name. I do understand that it will take a miracle for some forgiveness and a greater miracle to forget the pain and hurt inflicted on you by others, but that's where God comes in. The book will show you how.

I had just about completed the manuscript for this book when the evacuation of Americans and others from Afghanistan began. Then suddenly, there was a terrorist suicide blast that killed and wounded United States service patriots and others. President Biden declared that he would not forgive or forget those terrorists who perpetrated the heinous crime--they deserve to reap the consequences of terror.

Well, here I was completing a book on forgiveness—the type of forgiveness that Jesus demands of His followers. So I was figuratively shaken by the entire incident, and the President understandably called for revenge—perhaps called for justice. Then I reminded myself that even God Himself executed consequences on His people—even on David, a man after God's own heart. Then it became crystal clear to me that forgiveness or even unconditional love does not exonerate one from the consequences of one's unrepented and unremorseful infractions. So I added to the book a section on forgiveness with consequences.

I almost gave up!

When I saw all the hateful things happening around the world, I almost gave up on publishing this book. I questioned myself, how can I be encouraging forgiveness when there are so many reasons (excuses and rationalization for hate and unforgiveness?). I thank God that I did not give up. Because you are reading the book. May the forgiving God open your heart and help you to forgive others and help you to seek and receive His forgiveness!

And thank you for reading this book which I wrote just for you.

Blessings, love, and sincere prayer that no matter what the circumstances, you will forgive!

Chapter 1

Introduction

Forgiveness means different things to different people. As a Christian, my concept of forgiveness is based on my understanding of the teaching of the ultimate forgiver—Jesus Christ. One must forgive others if he or she wants God to forgive him or her. Jesus teaches His disciples-followers to pray, saying, **"And forgive our debts, as we forgive our debtors" (Matthew 6:12).** Luke's version of Jesus' teaching on the necessity of forgiving others before seeking God's forgiveness is stated in a more proactive manner, **"And forgive our sins; for we also forgive every one that is indebted to us..." (Luke 11:4).** A person who says he has no fault or has no reason to seek forgiveness from God will not need to forgive anyone. But there is no such person on earth.

You are reading this book; therefore, you already know about the importance of forgiving others, or you want to learn more or get a better understanding of forgiveness. In either case, the book will be beneficial to you. It is easier to talk about forgiveness than to actually forgive someone who has really hurt you. And it is much easier to tell a person that he or she should forgive someone than it is for you to forgive someone who has purposefully and deliberately abused or misused you.

However, as a Christian and a devout follower of Jesus, you must forgive others because you will constantly seek forgiveness. No true Christian will declare that he or she has no reason to seek forgiveness. Because all humans have sinned against God and more than likely against other humans as well. The great thing about forgiveness, as a Christian, you do not forgive just of your own volition. Rather, it is the Spirit of Jesus in you which makes it possible to do what is difficult—and seems almost impossible—forgive the 'unforgivable.' And as a Christian, you do not decide who is 'unforgivable'—that's a decision that only God has the right to make. So we will acknowledge that by your own effort alone—as sincere as you might be—it is virtually impossible for you to forgive someone for heinous atrocities against you, individuals you love, or society. But this is where the Spirit of Jesus in you comes to play.

You will appreciate the unfathomable forgiveness of God towards some whom natural humans might consider unforgivable. For example, God created the Garden of Eden and asked Adams to enjoy the Garden. He had the liberty to eat every fruit in the Garden except the fruits of one tree. Adams willfully disobeyed God and ate fruit from that tree. God was angry with Adams and his wife Eve. Nevertheless, God forgives them and makes temporary clothing to cover their nakedness.

In addition, God promised them a means for permanent coverage of their nakedness—their sins of disobedience ad rebellion against Him. That was forgiveness based on God's love, grace, and mercy. You will read about other examples of forgiveness that would be difficult or impossible for natural humans to do. Similarly, it is quite difficult or impossible for the natural human being, on his or her volition alone, to execute the types and number of times of forgiveness that Jesus demands of His followers.

Jesus is the Gate to Eternal Life: Forgiveness is the Key to the Gate

I have already mentioned in this introduction of this book that it is not because someone has sinned which will prevent him or her from getting through the Gate-Jesus to eternal life. Rather, it is because he or she refuses to use the combination key to open the door. Quite likely, you have heard the saying, "Prayer is the key, and faith unlocks the door to God's Kingdom." There is much truth in that saying; however, it misses a quintessential element to that combination lock. The saying misses the element of forgiveness. No one enters the Kingdom of God except through the Gate-Jesus. The four-element key to open the door includes the elements of forgiveness, prayer, faith, and grace. It is the element of forgiveness that is so elusive and often not fulfilled or attained by many individuals.

It should be clearly understood that forgiveness and unconditional love do not necessarily completely exonerate someone from all consequences of infractions against the Law of God or the temporal authority of the state. But a person who seeks God's forgiveness must forgive a repentant and remorseful person or persons for his or their infractions. You will read in this book how God forgives David for his serious sin but holds him accountable despite his pleading with God. You will read how Jesus forgives Saul (Paul) for persecuting His followers but holds him accountable. Even though the merciful God did not execute on David the full consequences of his moral and spiritual infractions.

So it is perfectly acceptable for believers in Jesus to have unconditional love for others and forgive them and yet hold them accountable. In fact, holding one accountable while showing unconditional love and forgiveness might very well be the best strategy to help someone get back on the right track or to just get on the right track.

This book explores incidents of great forgiveness in the Old and New Testaments and in the lives of ordinary persons. It stresses again and again that forgiving someone for egregious infractions can be difficult and seemingly impossible for a natural human being. But it provides the assurance that forgiving someone even for the most 'unforgivable' wrongs is possible through the Spirit of Jesus, who dwells in the born-again believer.

The book provides the assurance that one who forgives can boldly seek God's forgiveness and admission through the Gate-Jesus Christ. Jesus will lead that person to green pastures in the Kingdom of God. Read this book prayerfully with an open mind and allow the Holy Spirit to empower you; so that you will be able to do one of the most difficult assignments Jesus has given you—to forgive seventy times seven—as often as one genuinely and remorsefully seeks your forgiveness.

Chapter 2

Everyone Needs Forgiveness

The Bible tells us that God created a man named Adam and then created his mate, a woman named Eve. So even those who rebelled against God are still His creation. When Eve and Adam rebelled against God, God made the first physical garment for them to protect them from elements in the environment and to cover their physical shame; because all people belong to God even in their rebellious state. God does not pass the buck; instead, He shows ownership for even His most disobedient and defiant people. He is disappointed, though not surprised by their behavior. Nevertheless, God owns all.

All Souls Belong to God

God's special people—Jews in captivity in Babylon-- were complaining that they were suffering because of what their fore parents had done. They thought that they were reaping the negative consequences of the behaviors of their ancestors. They started to repeat the old phrase, **"The fathers have eaten sour grapes, and the children's teeth are on edge" (Ezekiel 18:2).** God instructed Ezekiel to admonish the people of Judah, who were captives in Babylon, to stop the foolish saying because the fathers, as well as their sons, belong to Him. Ezekiel records God's instruction in this manner, **"Behold all souls are mine; as the soul of the father, so also the soul of the son is mine: the soul that sinneth, it shall die" (Ezekiel 18:4).** The message was that God would be impartial to the parent and to the children. They were accountable for their own behavior, and God would execute justice to them—giving each what he or she deserves.

The key message is that all people belong to God, whether they do good deeds or evil deeds. Christians or anyone else does not get the option of deciding who belongs to God and who does not. Neither do they have the authority to decide who should receive spiritual life and who should receive spiritual death—that is God's business. The Minor Prophet Jonah could not comprehend or refused to acknowledge that even the evil Assyrians at Nineveh belong to God--Jonah wanted God to destroy them, but God wanted to spare them. They belonged to God, not to Jonah. God wanted the people of Nineveh to repent and turn to Him so that He would forgive them. They repented, and God forgives them and spares them. Jonah became angry with God for forgiving His own people. (Jonah 1:1—3; 3:10; 4:1—2)

God Takes No Pleasure in the Death of Him That Dieth (In Sin)

The faithful and merciful God does not take pleasure in the death of souls that are spiritually dead or in their physical death when they are spiritually dead. God has invested much in humanity. He created man in His own image and blew His breath of life in the first man-Adam. (Genesis 2:7). So God wants humans to be in close fellowship with Him. But He won't force them, although He will urge and encourage them and exercise a great deal of patience with stiff-necked and rebellious humanity.

When Adam and Eve disobeyed God and hid from God because their sin revealed their nakedness and shame--they deserved death (Genesis 2:17). But God sought them, forgave them with consequences—put them out of the Garden of Eden. But the mercifully made coats for them to cover their nakedness and shame and to protect them from the elements. (Genesis 3:6—9, 21). So even the God of love, grace and mercy, and forgiveness sometimes forgive but executes consequences.

God expresses His desire to see humans turn to Him in this manner, **"For I have no pleasure in the (spiritual) death of him that dieth, saith the Lord God: wherefore (therefore) turn yourself and live ye" (Ezekiel 18:32).** Ezekiel wrote this message from God to the Jewish captives in Babylon in approximately 571 A.D., fifteen years after Nebuchadnezzar and the Babylonians destroyed Jerusalem, including Solomon's Temple. The captives were blaming their ancestors for the just consequences of their rebellion against God. Rather than taking responsibility for the consequences resulting from their own behavior.

Through the Prophet Ezekiel, God sent the Jewish captives in Babylon a message of hope – He wanted them to repent, turn to Him, receive His forgiveness and live. They were His creation, and it pained His 'proverbial' heart to see them suffer and die in their sins.

Almost 600 years later, the Apostle Peter affirms God's desire that His people would turn to Him, seek His forgiveness and live. Peter puts God's desire for His people in this manner, **"The Lord is not slack concerning his promise, as some men count slackness; but is long suffering (patient) to usward (toward His people), not willing that any should perish, but that all should come to repentance"** (2 Peter 3:9). Often times, repentance is brought about through the instrument of chastisement. That happened over and over again during the time of the judges (Judges Chapters 1—21). The Apostle Peter makes it clear that God is patiently waiting to forgive anyone who seeks His forgiveness

The next time you feel inclined to criticize a rebellious not-yet Christian, it would do you well to remember that God is slow to punish, quick to forgive, and has an extraordinary amount of patience toward all of us. However, you should not take God's patience for granted. And remember that forgiveness might be accompanied by consequences.

All Have Sinned, And Come Short Of The Glory Of God

The title of this chapter is "Everyone Needs Forgiveness." Yes, you and I are aware of individuals—hopefully, they do not claim to be Christians—who proclaim that they never feel remorseful and have no reason to apologize or seek forgiveness for anything. Well, we should not excuse such persons on the basis that they do not know of God. The Apostle Paul reminds us that every human bean has an instinct to let him or her know that there is a higher authority—above all humans. (Romans 1:18). That instinct alerts each person to right and wrong regardless of culture or nationality.

So a person, even a not-yet Christian, knows when he or she does wrong and needs to apologize and seek forgiveness. From a biblical point of view, the Apostle Paul tells us, **"For all have sinned, and come short of the glory of God"**(Romans 3:28). A person who has never had any reason for being remorseful and repentant probably does not accept the infallibility of the Word of God as noted above.

When a Christian or a not-yet Christian acknowledges that he or she is not perfect—has sinned and has not met God's expectation—that acknowledgment opens the way for remorse, repentance, and God's forgiveness through His grace and mercy. So if all have sinned, are there consequence(s)? Yes, there are consequences, but God mitigates the consequences for those who are remorseful and repent. However, there are many who do not believe they need to be remorseful and repentant—because they feel they have done nothing wrong—and some do not believe there will be consequences.

The phenomenon of lack of remorse and repentance is not new. After Cain killed his brother Abel, God asked him, **"Where is Abel thy brother? And he said, I know not: Am I my brother's keeper" (Genesis 4:9).** Cain took no responsibility for murdering his brother. Imagine he was speaking with God, and yet he was defiant, disrespectful, and showed no remorse. However, God showed mercy toward him. God permitted him to continue to live. People in our times continue to be defiant of God's instructions; they do evil and are not remorseful or repentant as though they have impunity and there are no consequences for their behavior. Perhaps they are in denial regarding the existence of God and do not believe that human authority can hold them accountable.

David, the man after God's own heart, became remorseful and repented for taking Uriah's wife Beersheba and arranging for Uriah to die in battle. When Nathan confronted David about his wrong behavior, David proclaimed, **"Behold, I was shapen in iniquity; and in sin did my mother conceive me" (Psalm 51:5).** Then David prayed to God for forgiveness and asked God, **"Create in me a clean heart, O God; and renew a right spirit in me" (Psalm 51:10).** So the natural human being is prone to sin, even if he or she did not inherit sins from the first man, Adam, and the first woman, Eve.

David's remorse went beyond simply asking God to forgive him and clean him up. He pledged to God, **"Then will I teach transgressors thy ways; and sinners shall be converted unto thee" (Psalm 51:13)**. Sometimes remorse and repentance must be demonstrated by a 180-degree turn-around. Here David is pledging to assist others to turn to God and do right. One who seeks forgiveness should demonstrate genuine regrets and a commitment to refrain from doing the wrong ever again.

If David, arguably the greatest king of Israel—a man after God's own heart, as declared by God—admitted his wrongdoing and, in remorse and humility, sought God's forgiveness, how can any human being profess that he or she has nothing for which he or she is remorseful or for which he or she needs to seek forgiveness, even if that person does not acknowledge the existence of God!!

Any rational human being, even the not-yet Christian, must know that he or she has done something wrong intentionally or unintentionally and should be remorseful and seek forgiveness—especially when the wrong deeds or words are pointed out to him or her. There are consequences for wrong-evil deeds, words, and thoughts (sins). The ultimate consequence is noted below.

The Wages of Sin – Disobedience is Death

God, Himself clearly spells out the consequences of disobedience, to the first man Adams, in the Garden of

Eden. He gave Adams the authority and privilege to freely consume fruit from all the trees in the Garden of Eden, with the exception of one tree. God told Adam, **"But of the tree of the knowledge of good and evil, thou shall not eat of it: for the day that thou eatest thereof thou shalt surely die" (Genesis 2:17).** More than likely, God was referring to immediate spiritual death and eventually physical death> Regardless, God informed Adam of the consequences of disobeying Him.

It is well to note that God did not deprive Adam of his free will to make choices. God did not, does not want His supreme creation on earth to be robots; rather, He wanted and wanted them to think and use their free will to obey Him. God already knew that Adam would have disobeyed Him, so He told Adam the consequences he would face—immediate spiritual death and later physical death as well. Yet, as was stated, extended grace and mercy and apparently forgiveness to Adam and Eve. However, they suffered consequences—they were sent away from the Garden of Eden and had to work for their sustenance, and in time they faced physical death. No doubt, through God's grace and mercy, they have received spiritual life.

The Apostle Paul, centuries later, echoed God's warning in his letter to the Romans. Paul proclaimed the warning and concomitant good news in this manner, **"For the wages of sin is death; but the gift of God is eternal life through Jesus Christ our Lord" (Romans 6:23).** Well, since the first woman and first man–Eve and Adam sinned—all humans have committed our own sins. Some biblical scholars believe that humanity inherited the tendency to sin from Adam and Eve—this might be true.

What Does God Require OF Those Who Acknowledge That They Have Sinned?

When the Apostle Peter preached his first sermon on the Day of Pentecost—ten days after the ascension-- the risen Christ ascended into heaven—Peter proclaimed, **"Therefore let all the house of Israel know assuredly, that God hath made that same Jesus, whom ye have crucified, both Lord and Christ" (Acts 2:36).** The Peter who had denied knowing Jesus at His trial was a transformed person. The Holy Spirit in him bade him boldly. He spoke as a man with authority, not the timid

Peter who denied knowing Jesus less than fifty days earlier.

When the people heard Peter's declaration, **"they were pricked to their heart, and said unto Peter and to the rest of the apostles, Men and brethren, what shall we do? Then Peter said unto them, Repent, and be baptized every one of you in the name of Jesus Christ for the remission of your sins"** (Acts 2:37—38).

Repentance requires acknowledgment of being wrong about something; it requires being apologetic and remorseful. It suggests the idea of making a 180-degree turn-around in behavior, words, or attitude. Repentance suggests the idea of not just simply stopping doing wrong; rather, it suggests doing the right thing. The Apostle emphasizes God's expectation that those who acknowledge their wrongs should die unto their sins—give up doing wrongs as Jesus died for their sins---they should live unto righteousness—do the right thing. (1 Peter 2:24).

The Apostle Paul teaches that God expects that those who seek salvation must confess and believe in Jesus. He puts it this manner, **"That if thou shalt confess**

with thy mouth and believe in thine heart that God hath raised him (Jesus) from the dead, thou shalt be saved" (Romans 10:9). It cannot be stressed too strongly that the requirements of God which are previously noted apply to all who recognize God as Sovereign LORD and want to be saved.

In addition, God has requirements for those who have accepted Jehovah as their God and Jesus Christ as their Savior—followers of Jesus. The Prophet Micah summarizes God's requirements clearly and succinctly. **"He hath shewed thee, O man, what is good; and what doth the LORD require of thee, but to do justly, and to love mercy, and to walk humbly with thy God"(Micah 6:8)**. I often wonder how different our nation would be if our 'Christian' political leaders and many of our 'evangelicals' were following the admonition of God which was proclaimed by the Prophet Micah!

God still requires that those who are called by His name do good deeds, be merciful and humble themselves before Him. He expects His people to serve others in a humble, kind, and respectful manner. Unfortunately, many of those who professed to be followers of Jesus-believers are doing the diametrical opposite of what God expects of His people. But even so, the merciful God is patiently waiting and ready to forgive and forget the sins of those who sincerely seek His forgiveness—those who have forgiven others who have trespassed against them.

Chapter 3

Old Testament Models of God's Forgiveness

God Forgives, and Humans Forgive As Well

Throughout the history of humanity, God has been forgiving people for their infractions against His commandments and often for their deliberate rebellion against God. God has proven time and again that His love is unconditional and His grace and mercy extend to all nations and peoples. Not only does God forgives the infractions – sins of the remorseful and repentant, but He also forgets those sins.

In this chapter of the book, I select and discuss a few instances in biblical records when God forgives in fractions – sins committed against His instructions, against Him. In addition, I include instances when ordinary humans did the extraordinary thing of forgiving others. It is easy for God to forgive because God is Love and his grace and mercy extend from generation to generation. However, it takes something special for humans to truly forgive humans. It takes the Spirit of God dwelling in the forgiver. Some forgiveness is nothing short of miraculous, such as Esau's forgiveness of his brother Jacob.

Following are instances of true forgiveness in the Old Testament of the Bible.

The Greatest Forgiveness with Severe Consequences:
God Forgives Adam and Eve

The book of Genesis records the incident of God establishing the Garden of Eden and appointing Adam, the first man, as the steward. This incident was briefly discussed previously. God gave Adam the authority to eat the fruits of all the trees in the Garden except for one tree – the tree of knowledge of good and evil. God admonished Adam not to eat the fruit of that one tree. Adam had excellent fellowship with God and found delight in the presence of God. Then one day, the devil tricked Adam's wife Eve into eating fruit from the 'forbidden' tree, which God had strictly warned Adam not to eat from. Eve shared the (forbidden) fruit with Adam, and they ate it. God had clearly told Adam, **"for in the day that thou eatest thereof thou shall surely die" (Genesis 2:17).** Perhaps Adam had no concept of physical death and much less spiritual death. He was living a joyful stress-free life with daily fellowship with God. He took his good life for granted.

Well, Adam violated God's direct instruction to him and the trust God had in him. He was human with free will, and he exercised his free will contrary to God's instruction. He sinned-rebelled against God. He, some would say that his wife chose to obey the devil over God. He deserved the consequences of his rebellion—immediate death. But God spared him from immediate physical death. Later on, the Apostle Paul proclaims, **"For the wages of sin is death; but the gift of God is eternal life through Jesus Christ our Lord" (Roman 6:23).** Paul did not invent that rule regarding the consequence of infraction against God's instruction-sin. God had told Adam centuries before Paul's teaching that if he disobeyed God and ate from the forbidden tree, he would die.

But the God of unconditional love and endless grace and mercy intervened on behalf of Adam and Eve – He extended grace, mercy, and forgiveness to them. They received immediate spiritual death; however, God spared them from immediate physical death.

Although Adam and Eve received significant and extremely severe consequences for their rebellion against God's instruction – God ejected them from the Garden of Eden – yet God extended grace, mercy, and forgiveness toward them. God covers their nakedness, **"Unto Adam also and to his wife did the LORD God make coats of skins, and clothed them (Genesis 3:21)**. While God extended grace and mercy to Adam and Eve by making coats from the skin of an innocent animal, the animal had to die its blood was shed. This is the symbolism of Jesus giving up His life, shedding His blood to cover the nakedness and sins of humanity.

God extends grace, mercy, and forgiveness to Adam and Eve after they had committed perhaps the most egregious infraction against God recorded in the Bible. Yet the God of grace and mercy, who is synonymous with love, forgives them. And demonstrates

His forgiveness by covering their nakedness which was revealed as a result of their disobedience to God's instruction. However, Adam and Eve suffered serious consequences, some of which were passed on to humanity and by which humanity is afflicted in our times.

I cannot over-emphasize the point that although God granted forgiveness to Adam and Eve, He did not totally exonerate them from all the consequences of their sin-rebellion against Him. Certainly, God mitigated the severity of the consequences of Adam and Eve's sufferers. Moses records in Genesis that not only did God expel Adam and Eve from the Garden of Eden, but He provided measures to ensure that they could not reenter.

In addition, God pronounced a curse on the ground, which Adam would till to grow crops for his sustenance. God said to Adam, **"cursed is the ground for thy sake; in sorrow shalt thou eat of it all the days of thy life. Thorns also and thistles shall it bring forth to thee; and thou shall eat the herb of the field" Genesis 3:17 – 18**). Clearly, God forgives Adam and Eve, but He punished them and caused them to suffer great consequences for their sin—disobeying His instruction.

One point that must be emphasized is that Adam did not cause hurt and pain to themselves alone. Rather they brought hurt and pain to the entire earth and its inhabitants—humans, animals, plants, and the environment-- for a very, very long time.

Sometimes, forgiveness must go beyond mere words, such as "I forgive you." God's forgiveness of Adam and Eve softened the hurting of their mind and spirit. He covered their nakedness and shame and spared them from immediate physical death. And most likely, He spares them from spiritual death as well. God shows His forgiveness with His kindness toward the disobedient Adam and Eve. However, God did not exonerate them from all consequences of their bad behavior. He grants them forgiveness, but He expelled them from the Garden of Eden – tough love. He could not trust them with the tree of life (Genesis 3:23--24).

What would you do if you appointed a steward to take care of your property and gave him or her the freedom to eat fruit from any tree except from one tree? You told the steward that the fruit of that forbidden tree would be detrimental to him or her. But the steward deliberately disobeyed you. Would you be as merciful to the steward as God was to Adam and Eve and forgive that steward? Would you chastise him or her with grace and mercy and provide some measure of protection for the steward—protection from the elements and then dismiss him or her from your property? Or would you simply dismiss the steward without any concern for his or her future?

Well, God shows mercy, grace, and forgiveness to Adam and Eve, not just in words but rather in deeds. He sacrificed one or more animals to obtain their skins, which He used to make coats to cover the nakedness-shame of Adam and Eve in order to protect them from elements that they would encounter outside the Garden of Eden. This manner of forgiveness is beyond mere words, but there were also significant consequences. God killed animal(s) – shedding (perhaps innocent) blood – to use the skins for covering Adam and Eve, and He dismissed Adam and Eve from the Garden of Eden, with clothing made by God Himself, to toil to make a living for their sustenance!

While the emphasis of the foregoing discussion is on God's grace, mercy, and forgiveness, we should not underestimate the importance of recognizing the fact that there are consequences associated with sins and rebellion against God. Similarly, there are consequences for individuals who disregard 'accepted' rules of society, government, and the laws of nature or the environment. Sooner or later, those who disregard and violate the laws of society and the laws of nature will be held accountable—few will escape accountability

We are thankful to God for always intervening with His love, grace, and mercy to mitigate the full consequences of sinful behaviors of the remorseful and repentant person. And to forgive them/us!

God Forgives Moses With Consequences

Moses was arguably one of God's most dedicated and obedient prophets- and undoubtedly the greatest leader of God's people recorded in the Old Testament. Moses led the children of Israel out of slavery in Egypt and toward the Promised Land-Canaan for forty years.

He had great fellowship with God. He walked and spoke with God on a regular basis. Moses was meticulously obedient to God except on one notable occasion when the humblest human being on earth appeared to be arrogant. His behavior and words on this occasion were consequential and an existential threat to his life.

The Bible describes Moses as extremely humble. **"Now the man Moses was very meek, above all men which were upon the face of the earth" Numbers 12:3).** It is evident that regardless of what happened to Moses on earth, he was heading for the Kingdom of God.

Jesus, in commenting on the importance of humility centuries after the life and work of Moses, told the audience that they must humble themselves as little children in order to enter the Kingdom of God.

Moses understood the importance of humility and modeled it. Yet God held Moses accountable for one great error, even though He extended grace and mercy to Moses.

As the children of Israel were journeying through the wilderness toward the Promised Land, they needed water. On one occasion, God instructed Moses to use his rod (God's rod) to strike the rock, and water would flow from it. Moses obeyed God, doing exactly what God instructed him to do. And God provided water from the rock (Exodus 17:6 – 7).

On another occasion, the children of Israel needed water once more. God instructed Moses, this time, to speak to the rock so that God might provide water once more. By speaking to the rock, the children of Israel would hear that it is God who is providing for their needs. However, by this time, Moses was disappointed with the ungratefulness of the children of Israel; in fact, Moses was evidently angry with them.

So Moses gathered the children of Israel around the rock as God had instructed him, but rather than speaking to the rock, Moses said to the people, **"Hear now, ye rebels; must we fetch ye water out of this rock? And Moses lifted up his hand, and with his rod he smote the rock twice: and water came out abundantly, and the congregation drank, and their beasts also"** **(Numbers 20:10 – 11)**. Despite the fact that Moses disobeyed God's instruction to speak to the rock, rather than striking the rock, God provided water. Moses' greatest error appears to be that of speaking as though he and God were providing the water; rather than giving credit to God alone.

God provided the water. And evidently, God forgives Moses for his great error. Perhaps out of frustration with the rebellious children of Israel, the normally humble and restrained Moses behaved uncharacteristically, with what appears to be anger and 'arrogance' and suffered consequences for his unusual behavior.

In the age of transparency, let me remind you that this was not the first time Moses displayed seemingly uncontrolled anger as he led the children of Israel in the wilderness. God had called Moses to Mount Sanai. God gave Moses the Ten Commandments, which God Himself wrote on two tables (tablets). After forty days on Mount Sanai in the presence of God, Moses descended the mountain and found the children of Israel worshipping a golden calf. His own brother and co-leader Aaron had made the idol and told the people that the idol was the God that brought them out of Egypt. With righteous indignation and furious –uncontrolled anger, Moses threw the tablets with the Ten Commandments to the side of the mountain, breaking them into pieces. The Bible does not speak about God's response to Moses' display of furious anger on that occasion.

However, God held Moses accountable for his action of striking the rock and failing to give God full credit for providing the water. He would not permit Moses to put his feet on the ground of the Promised Land.

Moses Saw the Promised Land, But He Did Not Get There

Immediately after Moses struck the rock and God provided water, through His grace and mercy, God told Moses and Aaron, **"Because ye believed me not, to sanctify me in the eyes of the children of Israel, therefore ye shall not bring this congregation into the land which I have given them" (Numbers 20:12).** Think about it, Numbers Chapter 12:3, which was previously quoted, records that Moses was the humblest man on the face of the earth. Yet Moses failed to give God credit for the water in the hearing of the children of Israel. This error was a disqualifier for Moses and Aaron from entering the Promised Land.

Of course, in the incident described above, Moses acted contrary to God's instruction. He struck the rock rather than speaking to the rock. Moses' actions and misdeeds, as stated previously, were consequential. Evidently, God forgives Moses. But God held Moses accountable and executed 'some' consequences for his behavior. Nevertheless, he did not receive full consequences, which might have been immediate physical death and or spiritual death--instead, the merciful God mitigated the consequences-- and granted him mercy, grace, and forgiveness.

God's forgiveness of Moses did not extend to permitting him to enter the Promised Land. The place toward which he had been journeying for forty years. Moses led the children within striking distance of the Promised Land. God commanded Moses to ascend Mount Nebo. **"And the LORD said unto him (Moses), This is the land which I sware unto Abraham, unto**

Isaac, unto Jacob, saying, I will give it unto thy seed: I have caused thee to see it with thine eyes, but thou shalt not go over thither. So Moses the servant of the LORD died there in the land of Moab, according to the word of the LORD" (Deuteronomy 34:4 – 5). Moses viewed the Promised Land but did not physically enter the land. God had a better place for His faithful servant—a place of tranquility and peace.

There is no question that God forgives Moses for his errors. And perhaps Moses was ready for his well-deserved rest. Regardless, God did not permit him to enter the Promised Land, even though he viewed it and was so close to it. However, God granted Moses a special favor – never given to another human being, **"And he (God) buried him (Moses) in a valley in the land of Moab, over against Bethpe'or: but no man knoweth of his sepulcher unto this day" (Deuteronomy 34:6**) God demonstrates His love and faithfulness toward His dedicated servant, Moses. He took care of Moses his entire life--from the time he was born in Egypt when God protected him from Pharaoh's death squad to the forty years he shepherded his father-in-law Jephthah's sheep in the area of Mount Horeb to his forty-year journey leading the rebellious children of Israel in the wilderness--and at his death, God buried him on Mount Horeb.

One must be careful not to judge Moses too harshly for his error – his inadvertent 'arrogance,' apparent anger against the children of Israel, and for striking the rock in his anger and speaking as though he and God were providing the water. Rather, remember that although God was displeased with the action of Moses, He forgives him without removing all consequences for his errors. Similarly, God forgives the sins of those who seek His forgiveness with remorse and humility; however, God does not necessarily remove all consequences for their deliberate and/or inadvertent misdeeds.

It is an unfounded belief or teaching that when God forgives, He automatically removes all consequences for the infractions against Him or against others. The reference cited in Numbers 12:3 clearly indicates that even when God forgives a person for his or her infractions, He might still hold that person accountable--although with mercy and grace-- for his or her infractions--as He held Moses accountable.

This is the reason believers should always pray—seeking God for grace, mercy, and forgiveness--and asking God to mitigate the consequences of their infractions-rebellion against Him and against others. The good news is that once God forgives you--with or without consequences—He remembers those sins no more. God proclaimed through the Prophet Isaiah, **"I, even I, am he that blotteth out thy transgressions for mine own sake, and I will not remember thy sins (Isaiah 43:25)**. Because we are all guilty of sin, it is of great relief to know that when we confess our wrongs to God and He forgives us and removes our sins, He will no longer remember them. The writer of Hebrews expresses God's promise for those who repent and receive His forgiveness in this manner, **"FOR I WILL BE MERCIFUL TO THEIR UNRIGHTEOUSNESS, AND THEIR SINS AND THEIR INIQUITIES WILL I REMEMBER NO MORE" (Hebrews 8:12)**. When the Holy Spirit helps you to forgive others, you must ask He to help you to forget the hurt and pain as well. This requires a miracle.

God Forgives David, But With Severe Consequences

The Bible describes David as a man after God's own heart. When the Prophet Samuel conveyed God's message to Saul, the first King of Israel, that God had rejected him from being King over Israel because, **"Thou hast done foolishly: thou hast not kept the commandment of the LORD thy God, which he commanded thee: the LORD hath sought him a man after his own heart, and the LORD hath commanded him to be captain over his people, because thou has not kept that which the LORD commanded thee" (1 Samuel 13:13 – 14).** David was the new captain-King who God selected to be the second King of Israel-- a man after God's own heart. But David was a human being, and like his predecessor Saul, he committed egregious sins. He sinned against God, against a captain in his army, Uriah – who was leading a battle in the service of David-Israel – and against Bathsheba, Uriah's wife.

Nathan Confronts David for Sinning Against God and Uriah: Adultery and Murder

One evening, David was on the roof of his palace, viewing the scenery. Then to his 'pleasant' – perhaps unfortunate – surprise, he saw a beautiful woman taking a bath. David inquired about the beautiful woman and learned that she was Bathsheba, the wife of Uriah, who was a Hittite. David sent for the woman, had an affair with her, and sent her home. But she was pregnant.

When David learned that Bathsheba was pregnant, he tried to cover up culpability. He sent for Uriah from the battlefield. He tried to get Uriah to go to his house so that he could sleep with his wife Bathsheba However, Uriah refused to do so out of consideration for the other soldiers who were on the battlefield. He would not sleep with his beautiful wife on their comfortable bed in their cozy room while his soldiers were on the battlefield. He was faithful to his soldiers.

David's trickery of trying to convince Uriah to sleep with his wife – so that it would appear that Uriah had got his wife pregnant did not work. David went to a more drastic and caustic approach; he wrote a letter to Joab, captain of the army, and sent it to Uriah, ordering Joab to put Uriah in the front of the hottest battle and remove support from him. So that he would be killed in battle (2 Samuel 11:2 – 15). Joab did exactly had David had commanded him, and Uriah was killed in battle. Thus David had lusted after Uriah's wife, committed adultery, and was complicit in the slaying of his own faithful soldier, Uriah.

After Bathsheba had completed the mourning period for her husband's death, David sent for her and made her his wife. In time, Bathsheba gave birth to a son, which resulted from the illicit, adulterous incident with David. Perhaps David thought that he had gotten away with his heinous crimes of lust, covetousness, adultery, and murder. But not so fast. The Prophet Samuel records, **"But the thing that David had done displeased the LORD" (2 Samuel 11:27)**. God loves David, the man after His own heart, so much that more than likely, He would have given David any available woman David wanted to be his wife and requested of God. Would God hold David accountable or ever forgive him for such unnecessary and willful crimes?

God dispatched the Prophet Nathan to confront David about his terrible sins. Nathan admonished David, **"Wherefore thou hast despised the commandment of the Lord, to do evil in his sight? Thou hast killed Uriah the Hittite with the sword, and hast taken his wife to be thy wife, and hast slain him with the sword of the children of Ammon" (2 Samuel 12:9).** Nathan then pronounced severe consequences on David for his evil behavior, with the declaration of severe punishment for David, including that his neighbor would take his wives before his eyes. All this would be done in the open for the children of Israel to see.

David Repents, and God Forgives Him

When David received God's painful rebuke, which was delivered by Nathan, he did that which was characteristic of the man of God's own heart. He humbled himself and, with sorrow and remorse, proclaimed in agony and contrition-repentance, **"I have sinned against the LORD" (2 Samuel 12:13).** David accepted full responsibility for his actions--he did not play the blame game. Rather, he confessed that he had sinned against God. And God forgives him.

Immediately after David's confession, Nathan said to David, **"The LORD also hath put away thy sins; thou shalt not die" (2 Samuel 12:13).** It is conceivable, based on the words of Nathan, **"thou shalt not die,"** that God might have been contemplating physical death for David--an eye for an eye, a tooth for a tooth—as the Law of Moses requires. However, God did not execute the consequence of death on David. In fact, God forgives him for his sins of lust, covetousness, adultery, and murder. Nevertheless, he suffered significant consequences for unwise, unacceptable, and ungodly behaviors.

David Receives Consequences for His Sins

As stated above, God forgives David for his sins of lust, covetousness, adultery, and murder. However, God did not exonerate David from all consequences of his sinful thoughts and behaviors. The illicit, adulterous sexual encounter between David and Bathsheba brought forth a son. Although God spared David from immediate death, Nathan proclaimed that the child would die.

Nathan told David, **"Howbeit, because of thy deed thou hast given great occasion to the enemies of the LORD to blaspheme, the child also that is born unto thee shall die" (2 Samuel 13:14).** David definitely did not get away without consequences for his sinful behaviors. He was remorseful and repentant, and God forgave him and did not take his life. However, God determined that his child with Bathsheba would die.

David's behaviors in the incidents described above-brought consequences to him. But perhaps equally or more painful were the pains and sorrows which Bathsheba endured with the death of her child.

God caused illness to befall the child. David decided that he would do what he did very well-- he would pray and fast-- and so he did. He laid on the earth and fasted and prayed. God gave him no direct answer to his prayer. Nathan brought David no response from God. However, on the seventh day, the child died. That was God's answer--the answer was no-- the child would not live. He died. David received God's clear unspoken message, and he accepted it.

When David realized that the child was dead, he got up from the earth, bathed, anointed himself, and went into the house of the LORD and worshipped. Then David went into his house and ate. As long as the child was alive, David could pray and hope that God might restore health to the child, but when the child died, that hope was shattered – God had spoken with His action. God had executed a severe consequence on David by taking the child.

David willing accepted the consequence of his sinful behavior. God could have taken his life because of his sinful behavior, but God spared his life and took the life of the young child. God forgives David, but God allowed him to suffer some consequences of his behavior – the death of the child he loved so much. And there were other consequences, which David suffered as well.

It is well to mention, as stated above that undoubtedly Bathsheba shared in the consequences-- sorrows and pains, which were precipitated by David's behaviors. Interestingly, the Bible does not specifically assign blame to Bathsheba-- she might have been just a 'cooperating' victim whose beauty David refused to resist. David comforted Bathsheba and had sexual relations with her, and she got pregnant again. (2 Samuel 12:24)

God did not abandon the man after His own heart, nor did He cause Bathsheba to become barren. Instead, Bathsheba gave birth to another son and called him Solomon--**"and the LORD loved him" (2 Samuel 12:24).** Solomon succeeded David as the third King of Israel. God granted special blessings of wisdom, understanding, and wealth to Solomon. In addition, God permitted Solomon to build the first Temple for God – a privilege He did not afford to David.

The incident with David affirms that God is faithful and forgiving; however, He holds His people accountable for their behavior. But He extends grace and mercy to those who are humble, remorseful, and repentant. The incident affirms that God sees everything, even things that are done in secret. And He acts according to His timeframe and in His own manner. God decides if, how, and when He forgives and the consequences, He chooses to execute for wrong-evil doings.

God is truly merciful and gracious, slow to anger and ready to forgive, and plenteous in mercy. (Psalm 86:5; Psalm 103:8). A significant take-home from the incident with David is that forgiving someone does not mean that the offender is free from chastisement and rebuke-- all must be done in a spirit of love. I invite you to read Psalm 51 prayerfully and feel and internalize David's sincere, remorseful and repentant prayer as he pours out his soul to God. It is David's prayer after Nathan confronts him for his sinful behaviors previously discussed. May you/we be quick to repent, eager to tor forgive, and fervent in seeking forgiveness.

Jonah: The Defiant Prophet Who Would Not Forgive

In about 780 B.C., God gave the Minor Prophet Jonah an assignment to deliver a message to the people of Nineveh. The people of Nineveh were evil, and God wanted to warn them of the consequences they would suffer if they did not repent—imminent destruction of Nineveh. The message was clear and succinct. Unless the people of Nineveh repent and turn to God, God will destroy Nineveh.

At first, the Prophet Jonah defied God's instruction to go and preach to the City of Nineveh. He tried to run and hide from God. He wanted to see the City of Nineveh obliterated. As far as Jonah was concerned, the people of Nineveh--and the Assyrians, for that matter-- needed to be punished. Jonah surmised that the people of Nineveh were enemies of Israel; therefore, they did not deserve God's grace, mercy, and forgiveness. He did not want to preach to them because he did not want them to turn to God that God would spare the city. In effect, Jonah was acting as though he were God. He had a 'more righteous than thou' disposition-attitude.

In his attempt to run and hide from God, Jonah boarded a ship heading for Tarshis – the opposite direction to Nineveh. The ship encountered a catastrophic storm in the sea, and Jonah confessed that he was the cause. His 'getaway' ship was becoming a death trap for all onboard. The crew reluctantly threw Jonah overboard from the ship as Jonah requested.

Jonah, who thought that he could hide from or run away from God, probably thought that he would drown in the raging sea. He probably thought that he would prefer to drown than to preach to the wicked people of Nineveh. But Jonah could not drown because God gave him an assignment, and God intended to make him complete the important, city and lives saving assignment.

So God intervened and rescued Jonah from the raging sea. God provided a large fish that swallowed Jonah alive. While in the belly of the fish, Jonah prayed to God for deliverance and the LORD directed the fish to spew him out on dry land. (Jonah 3:1—10). By that time, Jonah must have realized that he could not run or hide from God.

God Forgives Jonah and Gives Him a Second Chance

Evidently, God forgives the would-be-defiant, running-away Jonah and gives him a second chance – a second chance which Jonah did not want God to grant to the great City of Nineveh. Jonah accepted God's forgiveness and gave a second chance to preach to the people of the City of Nineveh. Apparently, Jonah was a great and effective preacher – a man for God's mission.

Jonah Delivers God's Message to the City of Nineveh, the People Repented, and God Forgives the City

God's message was clear and concise, but frightening and yet offering the opportunity for mercy-- God's ultimatum and offer of grace, **"Yet forty days, and Nineveh will be overthrown" (Jonah 3:4).** In other words, Jonah delivered the message from God: "Repent, turn to God, stop doing wrong and being evil, or you will be completely destroyed." It is important to note that with God's warning of imminent obliteration, He also provided opportunities for the City of Nineveh to avoid annihilation. God extended His grace, giving them forty days to clean up their behaviors and receive mercy, grace, and forgiveness.

Jonah was the means through whom God chose to deliver His message to the City of Nineveh. Jonah reluctantly obeyed God and preached the same sermon to two-thirds of the City of Nineveh. Jonah was so obsessed with his anger against Nineveh and his desire to see it punished that on the first day of the three-day journey through the City of Nineveh, he did not preach. He started to preach on the second day.

Despite Jonah's lack of enthusiasm in delivering God's Message to the City of Nineveh, the people, including the king, heard Jonah's warning. They believed in God, humbled themselves before God, and fasted, repented, and prayed.

God was pleased with the response of the people of Nineveh to His message of the imminent destruction of the city if they did not turn to Him and stop their evil behaviors. So God forgives the City of Nineveh with its one hundred and twenty thousand people and its animals. The Almighty God forgives the people of the great City of Nineveh when they turn to Him and stop their evil ways. God forgives Gentiles—Assyrians in the great City of Nineveh.

Yes, God is a forgiving God and the Model of forgiveness; if it were not so, I would not be writing this book, and you would not be reading it. Because I would not be here and probably you would not be where you are as well.

As stated previously, God is eager to forgive and slow to punish. Centuries before the incident of Jonah, David, the man after God's own heart, declared, **"The LORD is merciful and gracious, slow to anger, and plenteous in mercy" (Psalm 103:8).** Quite likely, Jonah was familiar with Psalm 103 and knew that God would forgive and spare the City of Nineveh, and he did not want that to happen.

But think about the generosity of God's forgiveness to the Assyrians. God knows the past, the present, and the future. He already knew that within sixty years (722 B. C.) of the time, He forgave the great City of Nineveh--the Assyrians--they would conquer the Northern Kingdom of Israel and exile the people. Nevertheless, God forgave Nineveh, the capital city of the Assyrian Empire at that time.

God already knew how evil the Assyrians had been and how evil they would be in the future – even evil enough to destroy the Northern Kingdom of Israel in 722 B. C. Yet the God of the past, present, and future wanted to grant grace, mercy, and forgiveness to the City of Nineveh.

Vengeance Belongs To God: All People Belong To God

Vengeance or revenge belongs to God. It was not for Jonah to determine who God punishes or forgives. Centuries before the incidents of Jonah and Nineveh, God told Moses and the children of Israel, **"To me belongeth vengeance, and recompense…"** Deuteronomy 32:35). God extends grace, mercy, forgiveness, and justice/judgment in accordance with His will and timeframe. Everything belongs to God, and He does what pleases Him; therefore, no one has the right or privilege to question God's decision to forgive or to punish.

Some two hundred years after the incident of Jonah and the City of Nineveh, God instructed Ezekiel to tell the Jewish captives of Judah, who were in Babylon, **"Behold all souls are mine; as the soul of the father, so also the soul of the son is mine: the soul that sinneth, it shall die" (Ezekiel 18:4).** Then God went on to say, **"But if a man be just, and do that which is lawful and right....Hath walked in my statutes, and hath kept my judgements, to deal truly; he is just, he shall surely live, saith the Lord God" (Ezekiel 18:5, 9)**. The captives in Babylon were complaining that God was punishing them because of the sins of their ancestors and the sins of their children. That was not the case at all. They were being punished for their own sins. Yet God was ready to forgive them when they repented.

Jonah understood that God would have forgiven the people of Nineveh; however, he really did not fully understand the extent of God's unwavering love for all people; neither did he understand that all people – Jews and Gentiles belong to God.

Centuries after the incident of Jonah and the people of Nineveh, the great Apostle Paul in writing to the Roman believers--in Christ, reminds them, **"Dearly beloved, avenge not yourselves, but rather give place unto wrath: for it is written, VENGEANCE IS MINE; I WILL REPAY, saith the Lord" Romans 1:19).** So regardless of how someone has hurt you, do not try to revenge him or her. Instead, pray and leave the situation in the hands of the just and merciful God.

No wonder Paul teaches against vengeance. He persecuted followers of Jesus. Jesus forgives him, and he became the greatest advocate of Jesus recorded in the Bible. Nevertheless, he suffered consequences for his persecution of followers of Jesus. He himself was persecuted because he preached and taught that Jesus is true, the Son of God, the Messiah-Savior.

On the basis of his personal experiences, Paul makes the bold, unchallengeable proclamation, **"Be not deceived; God is not mocked: for whatsoever a man soweth, that shall he also reap" (Galatians 6:7; Romans 2:6).** God forgives Paul for his atrocities against the followers of Jesus. Paul made a 180-degree turn-around to God and continued 'straight;' nevertheless, he suffered consequences—flagging, imprisonment, torture, and finally execution by the Roman government—he reaped what he sowed. Yes, it is wise to leave vengeance and revenge and the application of personal judgment to the just God! The infallible and inerrant God knows how to handle every situation to achieve the correct outcomes.

You and I are not God, and you and I cannot, on your own volition, forgive others as God does; however, with the Spirit of God-Jesus in us, you-we are able to do what is impossible for the natural person to do – you are able to forgive even your worst violators – who you might ordinarily consider unforgivable. Because forgiveness sometimes requires an extraordinary miracle, which is possible only through the intervention of the Holy Spirit.

God expects His people to be willing and ready to forgive others as He forgives the people of Nineveh. And as He forgives our trespasses against Him. In a subsequent chapter of the book, I discuss Jesus' teaching on forgiveness and His modeling of forgiveness.

Chapter 4

Old Testament Examples of Humans' Forgiveness

A Model of a Man Forgiving His Brother: Esau and Jacob

If you are familiar with the biblical incident of Jacob and Esau, when you think of Esau, what first comes to your mind? Perhaps, you might say that he had no respect for his birthright. The birthright normally confers on the first son in the leadership privilege or responsibility of his clan-family or tribe.

Esau traded that honor for a little stew, claiming that he was starving to death. He bargained with his twin brother Jacob to exchange his rights as a first-born son— leader of his clan-- for just a bowl of stew. Maybe, you think of him as being callous, lacking integrity and appreciation for family tradition. You might even lament his foolishness in allowing the need for satisfying his immediate gratification to cloud his judgment. You might ask, how could someone with such a great future prospect do such a foolish thing?

Perhaps you might think of Esau as an unfortunate victim whose mother conspired with his twin brother Jacob to rob him of his special blessings. In that respect, you might admire him as a young man who loved his father dearly and wanted to please him and make him happy-- especially in what had seemed to have been the final years of his father's (Isaac's) life.

Esau was certainly a victim of his mother's partiality toward his brother Jacob He was also a son who wanted to please his father, Isaac. However, Esau had another profound godly characteristic – which is rarely mentioned when there is preaching, teaching, or discussions regarding the incident of Jacob and Esau. The often neglected characteristic of Esau was his repentant and forgiving heart, his attitude of kindness, and his display/behavior of love toward Jacob.

More than likely, you are familiar with the biblical incident of the birth of Esau and Jacob. They were twin brothers, but Esau saw the light of day–emerged from his mother's womb before Jacob did. Based on tradition, Esau had the right to be the head leader of his family-- in the succession of his father, Isaac. However, Esau went home from the field one day and saw his brother Jacob cooking stew. He wanted some so badly that he consented to Jacob's demand that he should exchange his birthrights for a bowl of the stew. The purpose here is not to evaluate Jacob's and Esau's behaviors but rather to state them as recorded in the Bible. It is not stated, in the Bible, whether the father and mother--Isaac and Rebekah—of Esau and Jacob knew about the exchange of birthrights for a bowl of stew. (Genesis 27).

Esau is Furious and Vows to Kill His Brother Jacob

Years after Jacob had taken Esau's birthrights, Isaac's eyes were dim, and he thought that the time of his death was approaching. He wanted his beloved son Esau to make him a meal of wild deer (venison), so he could eat a delicious meal and bestow his special blessings on Esau.

Isaac's wife, Rebekah, heard Isaac's instructions to Esau and decided that she would conspire with Jacob and steal Esau's special blessings. And so they did. In short, Rebekah helped Jacob to be an imposter – pretending to be Esau – and had Isaac bless Jacob rather than Esau.

When Esau became aware of what Rebekah, his mother, and Jacob, his brother, had done, he was 'justifiably' angry and filled with indignation. He swore that he would kill Jacob as soon as Isaac, their father, died. In a way, Esau demonstrates love and respect for his father and control over his raging anger against his brother. He did not want his father to go to his grave in sorrow, so he would wait until after the death of his father before he killed his brother.

Esau restrained, even though he purported in his heart to commit murder in the future. His behavior is a lesson from which we may learn much. When you are angry, try cooling off before doing something that you might regret. Someone suggests that before one says an angry word or does some revengeful act, 'count from one to ten,' and pray and sleep over the situation.

Esau Forgives Jacob

After Jacob deceived his father with the urging of his mother, he left his father's and mother's house as he fled from Esau. He spent twenty years working for his mother's brother Laban in Padanaram (Genesis 27 – 28). Jacob married Laban's two daughters and was now a wealthy man. He now wanted to return to Canaan, where his father and mother, and Esau lived. By this time, his mother, Rebekah, had died.

Perhaps, Rebekah received consequences for deceiving her husband Isaac and for causing Jacob to lie and deceive his father, Isaac. She never saw Jacob again after he fled from Esau.

Jacob started his journey home, but he was scared and terrified of Esau, even though God promised to protect him. Being afraid is a terrible consequence of sinning.

After Jacob had journeyed for a while on his way home, he arrived close to his father's home. He sent messengers with gifts to Esau to announce that he was on his way home. He had been gone twenty years. His gifts to Esau were another of his tricks. Evidently, the gifts were to soothe what he thought was Esau's 'justified' anger and his vow to kill him.

Jacob applied his usual trickery and executed strategies to prevent Esau from killing all members of his family and all his servants and animals if Esau intended to do so (Genesis 32 – 33:2).

When Esau learned that Jacob was on his way, he assembled four hundred men– not an army to attack Jacob--rather a welcome home party of four hundred men. Esau and the welcoming brigade went out to meet Jacob (Genesis 32:6; 33:1). Jacob was scared to death when he saw Esau and his four hundred men.

Jacob stepped ahead of the men who were with him and bowed seven times before Esau– a symbol of completion—perhaps an indication of respect, repentance, and remorse (Genesis 33:3). The once angry (twenty years ago) Esau responded to Jacob' entreaties, **"And Esau ran to meet him, and embraced him, and fell on his neck, and kissed him: and wept" (Genesis 33:4).**

It is well to note that Esau did not hesitate to let Jacob know that he had forgiven him. This is the greatest forgiveness of one man to another man recorded in the Old Testament. This was not a forgiveness of mere words; rather, it was forgiveness from the heart, which manifested with action.

That type of sincere forgiveness was not initiated in the Christian era. Rather, it was demonstrated by an Old Testament man, who arguably had good reasons to be angry with his deceptive and arguably thievery brother.

It is interesting to compare the immediate demonstration of forgiveness of Esau with the delayed manifested forgiveness of Joseph for his brothers. The incident between Joseph and his brothers is discussed later in the book. (Genesis 50:14 – 21).

Evidently, Esau had already forgiven his brother Jacob before Jacob tried to bribe him to forgive him. Esau initially refused to accept the gifts which Jacob offered to him. However, he accepted them because of Jacob's consistent and persistent urging. Esau demonstrated to all those present that he had purged himself of his anger, fury, and vow to kill his brother Jacob. Instead, he had totally forgiven him for his indiscretion-trickery toward him. Esau was a better person; he had rid himself of his anger and apparently replaced anger with love and forgiveness. This is model forgiveness that is worthy of emulation!

Reach Out To Those You Forgive

It is important that the person who forgives another reaches out to the forgiven one. Often times the person who needs forgiveness – the perpetrator of harm-- will withdraw from the victim because of shame or fear- being afraid or scared of repercussions. Forgiveness often requires that the victim or the forgiver makes the first step in making the offender aware that he or she has been forgiven! Of course, the offender has a responsibility and obligation to repent (apologize) and ask for forgiveness. However, a follower of Jesus, with the Holy Spirit dwelling in that person, is able to forgive even when the perpetrator does not seek forgiveness

It takes a person with a kind heart and the indwelling of the Spirit of Jesus to truly forgive a person for his or her infractions before the person seeks forgiveness. That is the type of heart that Esau had. No doubt, Esau had forgiven Jacob even before he knew that Esau was on his way home. You cannot force anyone to forgive you, and neither can you force anyone to ask for your forgiveness. However, with the Spirit of Jesus in you, you can choose to forgive anyone, regardless.

Cultivate Forgiveness

As Christians – followers of Jesus – you and I must strive to cultivate a kind and forgiving heart, as Esau demonstrated toward his brother, Jacob. Considering that Esau did not have the privilege of learning about the teaching of incarnated Jesus Christ on forgiveness (Matthew 18:21, 35) or the example of forgiveness that Jesus demonstrates, he was certainly a model of forgiveness before his time.

Esau did not hear or read the words of Jesus as He died on Calvary's Cross for the sins of the world, **"Father; forgive them; for they know not what they do" (Luke 23:34).** Yet he fully and completely forgives Jacob for his wrongs against him. You have read and heard about Jesus' forgiveness and His teaching that His followers must forgive others. So, forgiving others is not an option for followers of Jesus; it is a requirement.

Esau was an ordinary man. He was deceived twice by His brother Jacob. He was passionately angry at first; however, he did not allow his anger to consume him. Rather, he rose above his anger and feeling of betrayal and showed Jacob and all those around them the true meaning of love and forgiveness. Esau's forgiveness of Jacob was real. The Bible does not record any additional quarrel or animosity between those brothers after Esau's forgiveness.

Forgiveness is certainly, not only the key that opens to eternal life, but it is also the key to resolving conflicts and restoring relationships and fellowships among brothers, sisters, families, and nations—love always precedes forgiveness.

Joseph: A Prototype of Jesus – Sold Out By His Brothers

As a culmination of envy, anger, covetousness, and hatred, Joseph's brothers sold him into slavery, and the consequences were significant--both negative and positive outcomes. Joseph suffered unjustly—as a slave-servant, prisoner, and governor. God turned Joseph's unjust sufferings into immense blessings for nations and for family--including his brothers, who sold him as a slave.

Joseph had a 'right' to be angry with his brothers for the way they treated him. Not only did Joseph's brothers gravely violate him—selling as unwanted property, but they violated Jacob, their father as well. Joseph's brothers sold the seventeen-year-old Joseph into slavery, motivated by jealousy and envy, anger, and hatred. Then they lied to Jacob, their father, that the wild beast had killed and consumed Joseph. They claimed that only Joseph's blood-stained coat of many colors was recovered.

Favoritism Breeds Envy, Jealousy, Anger, Hate, Cruelty, and Lies

It was the coat that symbolized Jacob's special love for Joseph, which precipitated the envy, jealousy, anger, and hatred of Joseph's brothers for Joseph. Joseph's coat, the symbol of Jacob's love, had become a reminder to Jacob of the love of his heart. It also became the symbol that Joseph's brothers used to hurt Jacob and mock him. His sons had lied to him that Joseph was killed by wild animals, and they had Joseph's coat to prove it.

It was a fabrication; Joseph was not killed at all. Perhaps, Jacob was repeating the consequences of lying to his father Isaac (Genesis 27:18—25; Galatians 6:7).

Joseph Ascended to Power and Authority in Egypt and Provides for His Brothers and Father

After a series of unfortunate incidents, Joseph, who was sold as a slave in Egypt, accused wrongfully, and placed in an Egyptian prison, rose to become the second in charge in Egypt. Second only to the Pharaoh –

a governor. Perhaps, all this was a part of God's plan. As Paul teaches, **"And we know that all things work together for good to them that love God, to them who are the called according to his purpose" (Romans 8:28).** Many Bible scholars regard Joseph as a prototype of Jesus Christ—providing sustenance for his family and nations as Jesus offers spiritual life for humanity.

Joseph was wrongfully accused of attempting to rape the wife of Potiphar—one of Pharaoh's officers—and was placed in an Egyptian prison.

Through God's intervention, Pharaoh released Joseph from prison and interpreted Pharaoh's dreams. Joseph concretely predicted the seven-year abundance of productivity followed by a seven-year drought and famine that were imminent in Egypt and surrounding regions. Pharaoh appointed Joseph governor with absolute power to make and execute plans to address the impending situations.

When the Seven-year drought and concomitant famine in Egypt, and the entire region, including Canaan, where Joseph's father and his brothers were residing, arrived, all sought grain from Egypt.

Jacob sent his sons, Joseph's brothers, to Egypt to purchase corn. When Joseph saw them, he knew right away that they were his brothers, but they did not recognize that this 'Egyptian' official was their brother who they had sold into slavery years earlier.

After putting his brothers and his father through a great deal of trauma, Joseph finally disclosed himself to his brothers and sent for his father and all his household to relocate to Egypt. There would be another five years of famine on the land. Joseph wanted to make sure that his father and his household and animals were cared for – well fed and watered. So Joseph did the prudent thing – relocated his father and brothers and all their household to Egypt (Genesis 45:6).

Joseph Forgives His Brothers and Provides For Their Needs

Following the death of Jacob, after living in Egypt for about seventeen years, Joseph's brothers thought–and rightly so–that Joseph would have taken revenge on them for what they had done to him years earlier. Joseph's brothers were scared of what Joseph-- the powerful Governor of Egypt--might do to them. They quickly sent a messenger to Joseph saying, **"Thy father did command before he died, saying So shall ye say unto Joseph, Forgive, I pray thee now, the trespass of thy brethren, and their sins; for they did unto thee evil: and now, we pray thee, forgive the trespass of the servants of the God of thy father"** (Genesis 50:16 – 17).

The sins of Joseph's brothers had caught up with them. Their conscience was eating them alive, and they were scared for their lives. They were probably as scared as young—seventeen-year-old Joseph was when they sold him. They were reaping a 'mitigated' consequence of their evil act against their young brother, Joseph.

How did Joseph respond to this plea for mercy and forgiveness? He could have had them placed in the same Egyptian prison in which he spent many years as a prisoner of false accusation. However, when Joseph received his brothers' plea for mercy, **"Joseph wept when they spake unto him. And Joseph said unto them,**

Fear not: for am I in the place God?" (Genesis 50:17, 19).

It is most likely that Joseph intended to forgive his brothers along – and he might have already forgiven them as suggested by his statement, **"But as for you, ye thought evil against me; but God meant it unto good, to bring to past, as it is this day, to save much people alive. Now therefore fear ye not: I will nourish you, and your little ones. And he comforted them, and spake kindly unto them" (Genesis 50:20 – 21).** Joseph did put his brothers and, to a great extent, his father through some tense times.

Perhaps Joseph wanted to help his brother experience and appreciate what he endured for many years after they sold him; so they would be more considerate in the future. And maybe, God wanted Jacob to understand what his father Isaac endured when he deceived him and took Esau's special blessings—a reminder of the teaching of the Apostle Paul that whatever a person sows, he or she shall reap (Galatians 6:7).

In the end, Joseph was exceedingly gracious, merciful, kind, and forgiving toward his brothers. He even reminded them that God would fulfill His promise to Abraham, Isaac, and Jacob and lead them out of Egypt into the Promised Land. Joseph was so sure that God would rescue the children from Egypt that he had his brothers to vow that they would carry his bones with them to the Promised Land (Genesis 50:24). The writer of Hebrews lists Joseph among the faithful Old Testament honorees (Hebrews 11:22)

It is interesting to note that it was Joseph's brothers who initiated the plea for mercy and forgiveness. The brothers claimed that it was the instruction and command of their father Jacob before he died that Joseph would forgive them. Regardless of the validity of their claim, Joseph responded positively and quickly, and emotionally by forgiving his brothers. Joseph's brothers were remorseful and repentant for their despicable past attitude and behavior toward Joseph and toward their father. They sought mercy and forgiveness from the one who could execute justice against them or exercise love, grace, and mercy-forgiveness toward them. Joseph chose to extend love, pardon, and forgiveness to his brothers.

Joseph realized that perhaps God had orchestrated the entire incident, or at least permitted it, as a fulfillment of Joseph's dreams. Joseph forgives his brothers and goes far beyond forgiveness. He made it clear to them in words and deeds that he had forgiven them, and he assured them that he would meet their physical needs. He became a blessing to them and to their offspring.

There is no doubt that Joseph's forgiveness of his brothers was full and complete. Joseph, a prototype of Jesus Christ, anticipated and proactively subscribed to the previously cited teaching of the Apostle Paul centuries later, **"And we know that all things worketh together for the good for those who love God, to them who are the called according to his purpose" (Romans 8:28).** Yes, Joseph was a model of forgiveness. He teaches that sometimes God Himself might allow situations to come into your life so that you might be a blessing to others. So take the time to look for the good and opportunity for good in every situation which confronts you. And always be ready to forgive.

One of the most difficult things for the natural human to do is to forgive another who has done him or her egregious harm or has done harm to a loved one. Joseph forgives his brothers even before Jesus Christ died to endow humans with the Holy Spirit of forgiveness. Nevertheless, Joseph forgives his brothers for their evil deeds against him and against their father.

Believers in Jesus are much more able to forgive if they have the desire/will to do so. Because it is not the natural human who, by his or her own volition, is doing the forgiving. Rather, it is the transformed-born again person – the person who has the Spirit of Christ living in him or her who is able to truly forgive (John 3:3). As Jesus was quoted previously, **"With men this is impossible; but with God all things are possible" (Matthew 19:26).** Some things—even forgiveness--which are impossible with men are possible with God.

So, as a Christian–believer, a transformed, new person (created by God through Christ), you must trust the Spirit of Jesus to help you forgive the seemingly unforgivable—sometimes, it takes a miracle.

Chapter 5

Jesus Teaches About Forgiveness

The Disciples' Model Prayer: *And Forgive Us Our Debts, As We Forgive Our Debtors*

The Gospel, according to Matthew, records that there were great multitudes with Jesus, so He went on the side of a mountain and began to teach and preach to the people. This sermon or series of sermons became known as the sermon on the mountain. Jesus started this series of teaching-preaching with what was later called the Beatitudes (The blessed). Then He continued with numerous righteous principles and clarifications and expansion of religious laws/rules. He then went on to discuss the proper way to assist those in need—to do it privately and without boasting or fanfare.

Jesus then went on to teach the disciples about praying and illustrated a model prayer for the disciples. According to the Gospel According to Luke, it was the disciples who asked Jesus to teach them how to pray as

John (The Baptist) had taught his disciples to pray (Luke 11:1—4). Regardless, Jesus teaches the disciples a model prayer, which is more comprehensive in the Gospel According to Matthew than it is in the other synoptic Gospels (Matthew 6:9—15).

It is the portion of the prayer on forgiveness that is the focus of this discussion. Jesus teaches the disciples to pray to God, **"And forgive us our debts, as we forgive our debtors" (Matthew 6:12)**. Jesus knew that the disciples and His subsequent disciples-followers would violate God's instructions—disobey God—sin. Therefore they would need God's forgiveness.

However, for the disciples and subsequent followers to seek God's forgiveness, they would first need to forgive those who have done them wrong. Jesus went on to explain this requirement for asking for and receiving God's forgiveness, **"For if ye forgive men their trespasses, your heavenly Father will also forgive you: But if ye forgive not men their trespasses, neither will your heavenly Father forgive your trespasses" (Matthew 6:14—15)**. Jesus makes it clear that it is absolutely essential that you forgive others before asking

God to forgive you for your infractions or disobedience against His instructions

The Apostle Luke puts Jesus' teaching on the need to forgive others before seeking God's forgiveness quite clearly, **"And forgive us our sins; for we also forgive every one that is indebted to us...." Luke 11:4).** Implicit in Luke's recording is that by the time you seek God's forgiveness, you should be able to tell God that you have already forgiven those who have done you wrong. In other words, you are proactive in forgiving others. The clear message that Jesus taught His original disciples and teaches His subsequent disciples-followers-us is that forgiving others is a prerequisite for seeking God's forgiveness. Remember that true forgiveness is only possible through the Holy Spirit, which dwells in the true believer in Jesus Christ.

Forgive When You Pray: A Command, Not an Option

Jesus went to Jerusalem and went into the Temple and threw out those who were making God's House of Prayer into a marketplace of thievery.

The next day Jesus was teaching about having faith in God and asking, believing, and receiving. Then He turns to the important subject of communicating with God-praying. Jesus makes the declaration, **"And when ye stand praying, forgive, if ye have ought against any: that your Father also which is in heaven may forgive you your trespasses" Mark 11:25).** Three important points are made here. Firstly, Jesus expects His followers to pray. Jesus sets the example of praying regularly to His Father in heaven, sometimes publicly and often privately. Secondly, Jesus makes it clear, as I pointed out previously, that you must forgive anyone who transgresses before you even pray. Thirdly, and perhaps most importantly, the heavenly Father will forgive you if you forgive others.

Jesus' admonition suggests that even if you are not seeking God's forgiveness for any infraction against God, you are required to forgive anyone who has transgressed against you. And it is very unlikely that you have no known sin or unintentional sin for which you should seek God's forgiveness. The Apostle Paul quoting Psalm 14:1—3, declares, **"As it is written, THERE is NONE RIGHTEOUS, NO, NOT ONE" (Romans 3:10).** There is no doubt that since there is none who is righteous-sinless, forgiving others is a prerequisite for effectual prayers which God will answer.

Consequences of Unforgiveness

In continuing His teaching on forgiving, Jesus proclaims, **"But if ye do not forgive, neither will your Father which is in heaven forgive your trespasses" (Luke 11:26; Matthew 6:15).** Jesus explains the importance of forgiving by adding the blunt and consequential statement that your heavenly Father will not forgive you if you do not forgive others. If our heavenly Father does not forgive us, we are all doom—destined for damnation. Because we have all sinned and do not come up to God's expectations. **"For all have sinned, and come short of the glory of God" (Romans 3:23).** Further, as stated previously, there is none who is righteous-sinless. And there is a severe consequence for sin, **"For the wages of sin is death; but the gift of God is eternal life through Jesus Christ our Lord" (Romans 6:23).** Yes, we are doomed to eternal spiritual death—the wages of sin—but for God forgiving us of our sins as we forgive others.

Be Merciful And Forgive

On a previous occasion, Jesus was teaching a great multitude along with His disciples. He taught them that they must be merciful as their heavenly Father is merciful (Luke 6:36), and they should not condemn others that they would not be condemned (by the heavenly Father). Then He admonishes them: **"Judge not, and ye shall not be judged: condemn not, and ye shall not be condemned: forgive and ye shall be forgiven" (Luke 6:37).** It is noteworthy that Jesus appears to imply that forgiveness requires a non-judgmental and merciful disposition of the person who is doing the forgiving. In other words, a heart of love and mercy is necessary for true forgiveness. It is difficult to forgive a person who you are judging. In that case, you would be acting as a judge seeking justice rather than as one with empathy and love seeking to restore fellowship.

Even though you might think that the person does not deserve forgiveness, your heart of love and mercy overrides your judgment of the person, and you execute mercy and forgiveness; rather than executing judgment-justice. Of course, you cannot do this simply by your own volition and strong determination—you are able to forgive because of the Spirit of Jesus in you.

It is important to note that neither Jesus nor the Apostles ask the not-yet believer (not-yet saved) to forgive in order to be saved. The not-yet believer must first believe in Jesus and accept Him as Lord and Savior before that person has the ability—through the Holy Spirit—to truly forgive others as required by Jesus. Because only the new creation—the born-again believer is endowed by the Holy Spirit can forgive perpetrators and offenders of heinous atrocities against them and against others.

As a Christian, you and I have the Spirit of Jesus in us, which makes it possible for us to forgive even those who seem impossible for us to forgive. Because as Jesus told His disciple, **"With men this is impossible; but with God all things are possible" (Matthew 19:26).** As men—natural humans—things might be impossible for you; however, through the empowerment of the Holy Spirit, you can do the seemingly impossible.

Therefore as a believer, you must strive to have the same mind of forgiveness that was in Jesus as a righteous Man. **"Let this mind be in you, which was in Christ

Jesus" (Philippians 2:5)**. In another section of this book, I discussed how Jesus prayed that God would forgive those who were crucifying Him. He prayed, **"Father, forgive them; for they know not what they do" (Luke23:34).** As a believer-follower of Jesus, you must strive to have the same mind as was in Jesus the righteous Man—a mind that was ready to forgive.

To strive to have the mind of forgiveness which was in Jesus, the righteous Man requires the desire for such a mind and be willing to pray without becoming weary or discouraged. Jesus reminds us that **"Men ought always to pray, and not faint" (Luke 18:1).** If you desire to have the same mind that was in Jesus, the righteous Man, you must be prepared to pray sincerely and persistently.

Having a mind of forgiveness like the mind that was in Jesus, the righteous Man, will be necessary in order to forgive others as Jesus demands. Therefore consistent prayers will be needed. The Apostle Paul reminds us, **"Pray without ceasing" (1 Thessalonians 5:17).** And even fasting and meditating might be necessary in order that, through the Holy Spirit, you are able to do the impossible—forgive even those who commit the most egregious infractions against us. Jesus told His disciples that some miracles require praying and fasting.

If you have the desire to forgive as Jesus instructs us, the Holy Spirit will help you forgive. In fact, forgiving others is really not an option for those who are seeking to enter the Kingdom of God. Rather, it is a requirement instituted by God and emphasized by Jesus. So pray for a forgiving heart and forgive others as often as necessary—especially when they are remorseful and ask your forgiveness.

Forgive And Reconcile Before Offering Your Gift At The Alter

Jesus emphasizes the essentiality of forgiveness and reconciliation by telling the multitudes that they must forgive and reconcile before offering a gift to God at the altar. He puts His admonition in this manner, **"Therefore if thou bring thy gift to the alter, and there rememberest that thy brother ought against thee; Leave there thy gift before the altar, and go thy way; first be reconciled to**

thy brother, and then come and offer thy gift" (Matthew 5:23—24). Just imagine how shocked the Jewish people must have been when Jesus told them that they must reconcile with their neighbor before their gift to God would be acceptable! Reconciliation is a two-way street; it requires forgiveness as well as the acceptance of forgiveness.

Many Jewish people believed that they could earn salvation through their good deeds and by keeping the Law. Jesus makes it clear that forgiveness and reconciliation precede the offering of a gift that will be acceptance by God. In other words, internal forgiveness and reconciliation are significantly more important than external gifts, even when the gifts are intended for the church or for God.

Jesus expects His followers to do good deeds (Matthew 25:31—41). But their good deeds are not acceptable when there is unforgiveness in their hearts. In addition, it must be done with humility. **"Verily I say unto you, Inasmuch as ye have done it unto one of the least of these my brethren, ye have done it unto me" (Matthew 25:40).** Clearly, it takes humility to do good deeds for the least among us. It is a natural tendency of many to do good deeds for those who are least need such good deeds—perhaps with less than transparent motives.

This is amazing teaching of Jesus—nothing can substitute for forgiveness and reconciliation for those who want to enter the Kingdom of God. After all, Jesus paid the wages of sin—His death on the cross— that God may forgive you and reconcile to God. That's how important it is for you and me to forgive others and reconcile with those we forgive.

Please note that you cannot force anyone to forgive you; however, you can pray for them and leave the rest to God. But be sure you forgive anyone who has done 'ought' against you. And when you forgive someone, if possible, go the extra mile and do some good deeds for the forgiven person. His might be difficult for you, but remember that things which are impossible for man are possible with God—and the Spirit of God is in you.

Jesus Illustrates True Forgiveness: The Parable of the Lost Prodigal Son

Jesus uses a parable to illustrate true love and forgiveness. There can be no true forgiveness without love. It is the love of Jesus in the heart of a person which compels him or her to forgive with joy. The Parable of the Prodigal Son reveals the true love of the father for his once lost son, his forgiveness of his son, and the joy which fills his heart as he welcomes his son home.

There are numerous aspects to this parable that Jesus uses to illustrate real love and forgiveness. According to the parable (which seems so real—and if you listen to some preachers preach about the parable, you will think that they believe that it is a real incident). The certain young man in the parable thought that he had grown and wanted to leave home to explore and make his own life. He respectfully negotiated with his father for his inheritance, and his father gave him all that was due him.

The young man left home and had a great time sharing and using up the resources his father gave him.

Finally, he went broke, and there was no one to assist him.

With some degree of shame, guilt, and remorse, he decided to go back home and apologize to his 'waiting' father and seek his forgiveness. When the father saw him on his way home, the father ran and met him, hugged him, and kissed him. The father welcomed his lost son with open arms and had a great welcome home feast for him. The father told the servants, **"And bring hither the fatted calf, and kill it; and let us eat, and be merry: For this my son was dead, and is alive again; he was lost, and is found. And they began to be merry" Luke 15:23—24**). What great joy filled the father's heart! He could not constrain himself.

The father had no question for his son about how he had squandered his resources. He did not even give his once lost son the opportunity to explain his terrible experiences. Instead, he showers his son with true love and forgiveness. There is no doubt that their hearts—fathers and sons—were filled with unspeakable joy. The father demonstrated forgiveness, not just in words but in deeds and in a manner that the once lost son could see and feel. In addition, all those present could see and feel the love and forgiveness of the father and the remorse, appreciation, and love of the son as well. That is the type of love and forgiveness which Jesus expects of His followers-Christians-believers. Telling others that you love and forgive them is great, but showing them that you love and forgive them is greater!

There is no doubt that forgiveness begins in the heart, perhaps as a desire to forgive. Dependent on the infraction and the pains and hurt it causes, deep prayers, meditation, and even fasting may be necessary to transmute the hurt and pain and perhaps anger and a desire for revenge into a desire to forgive. The desire to forgive is based on the true unconditional love of Jesus Christ, which is in the heart of the believer. But it is the Holy Spirit that empowers you—the believer to summon the faith and courage to truly forgive despite the hurt and pain you might be enduring. Always remember that Jesus Christ does not ask you and me to do anything which He will not assist us to do. So rest assured that He will assist you and me to forgive; because He has instructed us to forgive. However, you must cultivate a spirit of forgiveness and pray always.

An Adulterous Woman Taken To Jesus For Judgement

Perhaps there was no greater sin a Jewish woman could commit in the Old Testament or in that the time of Jesus, in the eyes of Jewish men, than adultery. It did not matter if it were a married woman having an affair outside her marriage or a woman having an affair with a married man. In either case, the woman would be considered the perpetrator-offender and guilty of death by stoning. The only other sin that was close akin to adultery by a Jewish woman would be an open idolater—an open worshipper of idol gods.

Some scribes and Pharisees—Jewish men were certain that their accusation of adultery against this woman would pose a unique challenge—a trap for Jesus. They had caught a woman in the very act of adultery, and they wanted to test the genuineness of Jesus' teaching on forgiveness versus His adherence to the Law of Moses: **"Thou shall not commit adultery" (Exodus 20:14).** How would Jesus respond to their prosecution of this apparently guilty woman? No doubt, on the one hand, they would be ready to stone the woman if Jesus pronounced her guilty. Then they would turn around and call Jesus insincere in His teaching on forgiveness. On the other hand, if Jesus did not condemn her, they would quickly proclaim that Jesus did not adhere to the Law of Moses—He is a lawbreaker.

Those Jewish men—religious leaders just knew they had Jesus trapped. They placed the accused woman in their midst—the seat of trial and disgrace. **"They say unto him, Master, this woman was taken in adultery, in the very act" (John 8:4)**. Perhaps Jesus thought to Himself, where is the man? Certainly, she did not commit adultery by herself. Without a doubt, Jesus knew that those Jewish men, or at least some of them, would be accusing Him of sinning and crying out to crucify Him (Jesus) in a couple years or so. Jesus was not intimidated by these Jewish leaders. He simply stooped and wrote on the ground with His fingers—no response to the woman's accusers.

The accusers continued to press their charge of the crime-sin of adultery against the woman. No doubt, when Jesus stood, the men expected that Jesus would render His verdict. They did not fully understand that although he was the only One who was righteous and could render justice—He was not there as a judge—but as a Savior. As they eagerly way for Jesus's verdict with their prepared response, Jesus calmly gave a verdict, which was a non-verdict as far as they were concerned. Jesus softly said, **"He that is without sin among you, let him first cast a stone at her" (John 8:7).** I imagine that the silence and numbness among those self-righteous men were deafening and immobilizing. They must be credited for not faking that any was without sin because no one threw a stone at the woman.

Jesus Forgives The Adulterous Woman And Sets Her Free

Jesus already knew in advance the outcome of the incident, so he just quietly and patiently waited. After Jesus had asked that the person without sin cast the first stone on the accused woman, He stooped again. No doubt, the only righteous Man, the Son of God, on the scene was demonstrating humility by stooping and writing on the ground. And by this act of writing on the ground, Jesus was evidently sending the message that He—the Son of God is superior to the Law on which the religious leaders wanted to stone the woman. When Jesus stood, all the accusers were gone, but interestingly, the accused woman was the only one standing there. Evidently, she realized that Jesus had more to offer her than just saving her from stoning by the self-righteous religious leaders.

When Jesus saw that the accusers had disappeared, He asked the woman a rhetorical question, **"Woman, where are those thine accusers? hath no man condemned thee? (John 8:10).** The woman responded to Jesus' question, **"She said, No man Lord; And Jesus said unto her, Neither do I condemn thee: go and sin no more" (John 8:10)**. Not only did Jesus forgive the woman of her temporal-moral crime of adultery, which was punishable by death through stoning; rather, He forgives her spiritual infraction against God's Law. Evidently, Jesus forgives her for all her sins, something that the Jewish religious leaders could not and cannot do. Jesus granted grace and mercy to the woman and admonishes not to commit that sin (or other sins) anymore.

Jesus did not need to preach to the Jewish religious leaders, at the incident described above, on the virtue of forgiveness. He simply compelled them to examine themselves—self-examination. They were honest enough to realize and acknowledge that they had all sinned and fallen short of the expectation of God. They were their own judges, jurors, and witnesses. Jesus did not need to judge them. They judged themselves and found themselves guilty—perhaps even of adultery.

Sooner or later, they would seek God's forgiveness if they wanted to enter the Kingdom of God. Jesus demonstrates that God is ready to forgive sins—even sins that might seem unforgivable to religious leaders. Because things which are impossible with men are possible with God. Similarly, God will assist believers in forgiving infractions against them that the natural person might be unable to forgive.

It is important to note that although Jesus was not judgmental toward the woman and did not condemn her, rather, He forgives her. Nevertheless, He did not condone her behavior which was spiritually and morally wrong. On the contrary, He told her to go and sin no more.

Forgiving a wrong is not condoning the wrong. God's grace, mercy, and forgiveness should not be interpreted as condoning—accepting the wrong for which God forgives you, or the wrong for which you forgive a person, or the wrong deed for which you receive forgiveness. Forgiveness is an act of love that is non-judgmental and reconciliatory. Jesus shows how as an example for His followers.

Jesus Explains the Principle of Forgiveness to Peter

Peter asked Jesus how many times he was required to forgive his brother seven times. It was the Jewish custom that a Jew could forgive a person who offends him or her up to three times. Jesus had been teaching about the importance of forgiving others—similarly to how the Heavenly Father-God forgives His children.

The requirement of forgiving as the heavenly Father forgives was of grave concern to Peter. No doubt Peter understood the numerous times he sinned and would need God's forgiveness. So how could he forgive anyone so many times? He probably thought that if he forgives an offender seven times—the perfect/number of completions—that would be more than enough. So he raised the question to Jesus, **"Lord, how oft (often) shall my brother sin against me, and I forgive him? till seven times?" (Matthew 18:21).** Perhaps Peter was hoping that Jesus would ask him what the Jewish custom requires and then tell him to abide by the Jewish custom of forgiving a person up to three times or be generous and forgive seven times.

But Jesus' response was quite different from what Peter expected. Jesus essentially told Peter that he did not fully understand what He was teaching about forgiveness. Peter was probably willing to consider the Jewish tradition of forgiving a person up to three times, and he was willing to go beyond tradition to seven times. But his question to Jesus implies that he thought that forgiving a person seven times was quite much, and to forgive a person more than seven times was beyond his ability or even beyond his desire. Therefore it must have been a real bombshell when Jesus said to Peter, **"I say not unto thee, Until seven times: but, Until seventy times seven" (Matthew 18:22).** Jesus was explaining to Peter that he should forgive a person as often as that person offends him and seeks forgiveness. In other words, do not keep a record of the offenses. Just forgive when the offender repents and seeks forgiveness. In subsequent chapters of the book, I discuss how Jesus and Stephen forgive offenders who did not even seek their forgiveness.

If you desire that God forgives your trespasses against Him when you repent and seek His forgiveness, you must be willing to forgive those who offend or violate you and repent and seek your forgiveness. As Christians-believers, we must guard against using the 'unconverted' Peter's criterion when we think of love and forgiveness. Peter thought that he was doing more than enough in forgiving someone of his or her infractions seven times because the Jewish custom requires forgiveness three times.

However, Jesus' requirement is for His followers to love everyone, even the enemy, at all times and to forgive as often as the offender seeks forgiveness. Jess asks His followers to do things that are impossible for the natural person to do. He said to His followers, **"The things which are impossible with men are possible with**

God" (Luke 18:24). If we only want to do the things which are possible with men, then we don't really need Jesus-the empowerment of the Holy Spirit. Because the Spirit of God/Jesus is in the believer, he or she is able to do the impossible—forgive others.

Jesus, Himself, did not wait for the offenders to seek forgiveness before He forgives them. In a subsequent section of the book, I discuss how Jesus forgives His murderers while He was dying on Calvary's Cross to make eternal life possible for all who believe in Him.

Forgive the Repentant Person as Often as He Seeks Forgiveness

Jesus teaches His disciples that they should be careful to guard their behavior—be careful not to offend any of His followers, especially children (physical and spiritual immature). Then He declares, **"If thy brother trespass against thee, rebuke him; and if he repent, forgive him" (Luke 17:3).** Alexander Pope is credited with the saying, "To err is human, to forgive is divine." Even the greatest of saints make errors because they are human. Implicit in Jesus' admonition is a requirement that those who are corrected for their errors should be remorseful and repent.

Interestingly, as stated previously, Jesus forgives His murderers who did not repent and seek His forgiveness at the time they were murdering Him. Perhaps Jesus anticipated that His murderers would repent and seek God's forgiveness. In forgiving His murderers while they were in the process of murdering Him—fulfilling God's plan of sacrificing His Son—Jesus demonstrates the incomprehensible extent of His forgiveness to humanity, based on the unconditional love of God and the love of Jesus.

The great Apostle Paul expressed his need for forgiveness in his remarks that when he tried to do good, evil was always present itself, **"I find then a law, that, when I would do good, evil is present with me" (Roman 7:21).** So even the best of believer-follower of Jesus makes mistakes. Jesus knows that, so He provides a way to deal with those who make errors and are remorseful and repentant. Jesus says that the believer should correct the person who is in error and forgive the person if he or she repents. No one should deliberately make errors, but those who make errors should be quick in accepting responsibility and quick to repent, and eager for restoration into fellowship with other believers.

As you think of the remorseful repentant, you can divide them into two categories. The first category includes those who are repenting for their sins and accepting Jesus Christ as their Lord and Savior. They are becoming believers in Jesus—new creatures born again. The second category of remorseful repentant includes believers who have erred—committed infractions by what they did, what they failed to do, or what they said or failed to say. The admonition which Jesus proclaims regarding forgiveness is applicable to both categories of the remorseful repentant. However, in our context, it appears to be directed to those who believe in Jesus.

Those of us who believe in Jesus must forgive others before seeking God's forgiveness, or God will not forgive our trespasses-infractions. Jesus' instruction is plain and straightforward: Forgive others!

Chapter 6

The Greatest Demonstration Of Forgiveness By The God-Man: Jesus!

Jesus Is The Gate, And Forgiveness Is The Key To God's Kingdom

I have shared-preached a sermon on forgiveness on many occasions at churches and with inmates at a correctional facility. I usually begin my presentation by declaring that it is not because a person has sinned that prevents him or her from entering the Kingdom of God. Then I pause for a few moments and continue, **"For all have sinned, and come short of the glory of God" (Romans 3:23).** And I usually get a lot of Amens! Then I usually explain that if everyone who sins is denied access to the Kingdom of God, the only Man (God-Man) who could enter would be Jesus Christ. Jesus Christ is the only Man who walked on earth and did not sin. These include people such as Enoch, Noah, Abraham, Moses, David,

Elijah, Zacharias, Simeon, John the Baptist, the Apostle Paul, and others. They all sinned!

So, I proclaim that sin will prevent you from entering the Kingdom of God; however, it is not simply because you have sinned. Remember, Paul, arguably the greatest apostle informs us that everyone has sinned. In addition, Paul informs us that "When I (Paul) would do good, **evil is present with me (him)" (Romans 7:21).** Toward the end of his life, nearing his execution, Paul told Timothy, **"I have fought a good fight, I have finished my course, I have kept the faith: henceforth there is laid up for me a crown of righteousness, which the righteous judge, shall give me on that day: and not to me only, but unto all them also that love his appearing" 2 Timothy 4:7—8).** Paul (Saul) had sinned greatly. He had persecuted followers of Jesus and aided and abetted others in the stoning of Deacon Stephen and other followers of Jesus Christ.

Yet Paul was confident that he would enter the Kingdom of God and receive a crown of righteousness. His past sins did not block him from the Kingdom of God. He repented of his past sins. Jesus forgave him. In addition, Jesus commissioned him to be an evangelist, especially to the Gentile nations, which he formally despised.'

Jesus Is The Gate, And Forgiveness Is The Key To The Kingdom Of God

If you have been around church people, you have probably heard the saying that "Prayer is the key, and faith unlocks the door to the Kingdom of God." The saying is not without some merit since prayer and faith are both necessary elements to enter the Kingdom of God. However, in this context, I proclaim that Jesus Christ is the gate—door and forgiveness is the ticket that carries you into the Kingdom of God. There is no question about the importance of prayer—the prayer seeking forgiveness-- in order to enter the Kingdom of God. Because all have sinned, and the wages of sin is death—spiritual death.

Therefore, since all have sinned and deserve the wages of sin—death, a person can only escape death—the wages of sin by forgiveness. Forgiveness begins with the person who is guilty of an infraction called sin.

Remember, Jesus teaches in the Disciples' Model Prayer that a person who desires God's forgiveness must first forgive those who have done him or her wrong. Then and only then can such a person seek God's forgiveness. And God's forgiveness is necessary for anyone who desires to enter the Kingdom of God. Yes, faith is essential to enter the Kingdom of God. Paul teaches that **"For by grace are ye saved through faith: and that not of yourselves: it is the gift of God: and not by works lest any man should boast" (Ephesians 2:8—9)**.

Prayer is necessary for seeking God's forgiveness, and faith is essential to believe and access God's forgiveness. And your forgiving others who have wronged you is quintessential before you can ask God for His forgiveness for your misdeeds against your neighbor and against God. So, I argue that your greatest block from going through the narrow gate—door (Jesus Christ) into the Kingdom of God is the failure or refusal to apply the ticket—forgiveness.

Jesus: The Personification Of Forgiveness

Jesus taught His disciples the model prayer, which is a succinct yet complete prayer. However, skeptics were not sure that Jesus would demonstrate the type of forgiveness He had been teaching—forgiving someone for an egregious crime and not holding him or her accountable. As discussed previously, God forgives Adam for disobeying His instruction, but God did not exonerate Adam from all consequences of his rebellion against Him. He expelled Adam and Eve from the Garden of Eden. So how would Jesus exemplify the type of 'unconditional' forgiveness He had been expounding and urging?

Jesus waited until He allowed Himself to be most flagrantly violated before He demonstrated His transformational forgiveness to the worst of worst—seemingly unforgivable. This was and is life-transforming forgiveness because only God's forgiveness can transmute a person from the brink of eternal death and damnation to eternal life—and Jesus wanted the transformation of His enemies. Because Jesus is the personification of forgiveness.

Jesus Forgives His Murderers

Jesus was executed on Calvary's Cross because of willful, blatant, and deliberate
miscarriage of justice by Jewish religious leaders and Roman accomplices. He still had all power in His hand to destroy those who knew that He was innocent of the fake charges against Him. And yet, rather than asking His Father for justice-judgment for His murderers, He asks for mercy for them. Jesus looked beyond the hate, jealousy, self-righteousness, and vindictiveness of His murderers and saw their abject shame, the trajectory for complete destruction, and their need. Jesus saw their need for pity, compassion, and forgiveness. They had no shame or compassion.

The murderers at the cross did not humble themselves and ask Jesus for help. They were overtaken by hate, hardness of heart, and cruelty. Nevertheless, Jesus Christ, the Son of God, looks beyond their ignorance and self-righteousness and cries out to His Father on behalf of His misguided executioners.

Jesus cries out, **"Father, forgive them: for they know not what they do" (Luke 23:34).** Certainly, they should have known that they were executing an innocent Man, even if they did not believe that He is the Son of God. And some of the religious leaders may have intellectually known that Jesus is the Son of God. But they could not get themselves to accept Jesus as the Son of God. Sadly, many may not have known that they were fulfilling prophecies of the Old Testament as well as the predictions of Jesus regarding His death.

Note that Jesus prays (out loud) to God to forgive His wretched murderers. He wanted them to hear His prayer for their forgiveness. Certainly, Jesus had the authority to forgive them quietly, but He wanted them to know that He was praying for their forgiveness. Many of them knew about God, and many might have even believed in God, but they could or would not allow themselves to believe in Jesus. Nevertheless, their heinous crime against the Son of God did not alter Jesus' unconditional love for them. Jesus extended grace to the 'unforgivable' by forgiving them.

Jesus' forgiveness means that the guilty ones would not need to live with guilt and shame for a long time if they were humble enough to accept Jesus' forgiveness.

What a model of not just teaching about forgiveness, but rather showing forgiveness. It is this type of forgiveness God provides which allows repented sinners—believers in Jesus Christ-- to gain entrance to the Kingdom of God. Those who accept God's forgiveness enter His Kingdom through the narrow gate—Jesus Christ. In addition, it is that type of forgiveness that Jesus expects of His followers. This is possible only through the Spirit of Jesus, which lives in believers. As stated previously, Jesus is indeed the personification of forgiveness—the model--who believers must emulate.

Jesus Forgives The Criminal Dying On The Cross And Grants Him Salvation

Not only did Jesus forgives His executioners, but He also forgave a criminal who was being crucified on a cross adjacent to His. The criminal dying on his cross confessed that he was duly receiving the consequence of his criminality. He even chastised another criminal, who was being crucified beside him, for being disrespectful toward Jesus. **"And he said unto Jesus, Lord, remember me when thou comest into thy kingdom" (Luke 23:42).** Evidently, Jesus forgives this man's sins instantaneously. Because the man had confessed that he was guilty of wrongful deeds. Jesus told him that he would be with Him Jesus that day.

Since no one with unforgiven sins can enter the Kingdom of God, as stated previously, Jesus must have forgiven the dying criminal instantaneously. Jesus responded to his request in this manner, **"Verily I say unto thee, to day shalt thou be with me in paradise" (Luke 23:43).** Imagine Jesus is being executed by Jewish religious leaders and Roman accomplices, yet Jesus takes the time to forgive a criminal-a murderer who was receiving the wages of sin-physical and spiritual death. And not only did Jesus forgives him, but he promised him that he would be with Jesus in paradise on that very day.

While Jesus-the righteous Man-Son of God, was experiencing physical death--He forgave the sins of--and gave spiritual-eternal life to--a remorseful and repentant criminal whose death was imminent. As Christians, you and I must be willing and ready to forgive those who hurt us, even in difficult situations. But again, such an ability to forgive is impossible of your own volition. It is the Spirit of Christ in you which makes it possible for you to forgive the 'hard' to forgive. Jesus had told his disciples, **"The things which are impossible with men are possible with God" (Luke 18:27).** When the Spirit of Jesus is in us, we are willing and able to forgive, and we strive daily to have a similar mind that was in Jesus, the righteous Man-Son of God.

The Apostle Paul reminds us, **"Let the same mind be in you (us) which was also in Christ Jesus (the righteous Man)" (Philippians 2:5).** When Christians have the same mind which was in Christ Jesus—the righteous Man-- we have the desire to forgive, and the Spirit of Jesus empowers us to forgive even the seemingly 'unforgivable'-- impossible to forgive. It is the Spirit of Jesus working in the Christian believer which empowers him or her to forgive. But it all starts with the desire to forgive.

Each person—Christian-believer and not-yet believer still has the free will to desire to forgive or not to forgive. Do you have a desire to forgive someone, anyone? Jesus forgives the criminal dying on the cross, as well as those who were crucifying Him. Jesus knows what it means and takes to forgive even the seemingly unforgivable. He will help you--a believer, to forgive others-- if you have the desire to forgive and you ask and trust Him to assist you. You must forgive so that god will forgive you when you ask.

Chapter 7

The First Act Of Forgiveness Of The Risen Jesus And His Assignment To His Betrayer Peter

Jesus Predicts His Desertion: Peter Takes Offence

Jesus and His disciples completed His (their) Last Supper in the upper room. This would be the initiation of the First Memorial Lord's Supper. **"And when they had sung a hymn, they went out into the mount of Olives" (Matthew 26:30).** Jesus continued His teaching and predictions about His death while He and His disciples were at Mount Olives. Jesus then makes a proclamation. **"Then Jesus said unto them, All ye shall be offended because of me this night: for it is written, I WILL SMITE THE SHEPHERD, AND THE SHEEP OF THE FLOCK SHALL BE SCATTERED ABROAD" (Matthew 26:31).** Peter was really up in arms when Jesus made the prediction that the disciples would be offended and abandon Him. No doubt,

Peter was especially offended that Jesus thought that he—Peter, the one who loved Jesus so much would ever disassociate from Jesus under any circumstance. Peter probably thought that he could have remained faithful to Jesus of his own volition, determination, and rugged fisherman tenacity—his intention was good.

Peter was 'cock' sure that he was ready to stay with Jesus and even ready to die for and with Jesus. To Jesus' prediction, **"Peter answered and said unto him, Though all men shall be offended because of thee, yet will I never be offended" (Matthew 26:33).** Peter was confident in his own strength and determination to stay hang with Jesus regardless of the situation. **"Jesus said unto him, Verily I say unto thee, That this night, before the cock crow, thou shalt deny me thrice" Matthew 26:34).** By this time, Peter had been a member of Jesus' inner circle, Jesus, for three years. He should have understood that Jesus' prediction would have come true—His words would not return void unless Jesus intercedes to change them.

Nevertheless, Pete, who thought that he could do anything of his own volition, buckled down instead of asking Jesus to intercede on his behalf. On the basis of his own strength and seemingly unwavering commitment to Jesus, **"Peter said unto him, Though I should die with thee, yet will I not deny thee. Likewise also said all the disciples" Matthew 26:35).** There is no question that Peter had every intention to stay with Jesus and to defend and fight for Him. However, as one of my teachers was known to say, "The road to hell is paved with good intentions." Peter, of his own volition, could not handle the possibility of being crucified with Jesus or even being punished on behalf of Jesus. That was simply too much for him to bear.

The Jewish Religious Leaders Arrest Jesus, And Peter Denies Him

Jesus and eleven of His disciples left Mount Olives and went to Gethsemane, where Jesus prayed three times, asking God to remove the cup of death on the cross from Him if it was God's will. Shortly thereafter, Jesus was arrested by the religious leaders with the assistance of Roman soldiers. The soldiers led Jesus away to **"Caiaphas, the high priest where the scribes and the elders were assembled" (Matthew 26:57).**

Peter Denies Knowing Jesus

Peter, who had committed to die with Jesus, followed the arresting mob far behind to the high priest's palace. He wanted to see what would happen to Jesus. Peter sat as an observer in the back of the palace. Individuals in the priest's palace identified Peter as a follower of Jesus. Peter denied that he even knew Jesus and what they were talking about.

The third time that Peter was confronted, he was told that his accent revealed that he was with Jesus. **"Then began he (Peter) to curse and to swear, saying, I know not the man, and immediately the cock crew" (Matthew 26:74).** Peter, one of Jesus' inner circle disciples and arguably the spokesperson for the disciples, denied knowing Jesus three times within a short period of time. Matthew records that Peter remembered the words of Jesus to Peter, **"Before the crow, thou shalt deny me thrice. And he went out and wept bitterly" (Matthew 26:75).** Was it over for Peter? Judas betrayed Jesus once and hanged himself. Peter had three opportunities to acknowledge that he was not just a follower but rather a chosen disciple—a member of Jesus' inner circle. He wept bitterly. What would he do with himself? Would he follow the example of Judas, who hanged himself? Perhaps, more importantly, what would Jesus do with Peter?

Jesus Reaches Out To Peter

Jesus was crucified on Calvary's Cross. By this time, Judas had committed suicide because of his feeling of guilt for betraying Jesus. On the third day of Jesus' crucifixion, the day after the Sabbath, some women went to the tomb to anoint Jesus' body for His permanent burial. They were astonished by what they discovered. Jesus' body was not in the tomb. He had risen from the dead and had left the tomb. There was an angel sitting at the sepulcher (tomb), who invited the women to inspect for themselves the place where Jesus was laid. Then the angel instructed them, **"But go your way, tell the disciples and Peter that he (Jesus) goeth before you into Galilee: there shall ye see him, as he said unto you" (Mark 16:7).** Angels do not make decisions on their own, they are messengers of God—Jesus. So, the angel who spoke to the women at the sepulcher was simply delivering the message which Jesus had given him. Go tell Peter and others.

Jesus Forgives Peter And Gives Him A Special Assignment

Jesus wanted to assure Peter that although he had slipped and fallen, Jesus had not given up on him. Jesus wanted Peter to be with the other disciples when He met them in Galilee. Jesus wanted Peter to know that He had forgiven him for denying Him. Jesus had already told the disciples in Gethsemane that their hearts were willing, but their flesh was weak. Jesus reached out specifically to Peter by name and told him to meet Him in Galilee.

Jesus had forgiven a dying thief on the cross and His murderers while He was dying on the cross; therefore, He was more than ready to forgive His friend, Peter, who had slipped and fell. The never to die again Messiah was eager to forgive His disciple Peter for denying Him three times in a short space of time.

Jesus Restores Peter

But Jesus did more than forgive Peter for denying Him. Jesus restores Peter to a prominent place in His earthly ministry—taking care of Jesus' sheep. On His third appearance to the disciples after Jesus rose from the dead, the disciples were at the sea of Tiberias fishing. They were fishing all night but caught no fish. In the morning, Jesus stood by the shore; however, the disciples did not recognize Him, Jesus told them to cast their net, and they caught one hundred ad fifty-three large fishes (John 21:6—9).

Jesus Asks Peter The Fish Questions About Love

Jesus prepared fish from the catch and bread which He made/procured. He invited the disciples to dine. When they were dining, Jesus asked Simon Peter, **"Simon, son of Jonas, lovest thou me more than these" (John 21:15).** Jesus asked Peter if he loved Jesus more than he loved the fishes. Peter was once a fisherman, and it would not be too difficult for him to revert to his original occupation as a fisherman. Peter responded that he loved Jesus. Jesus told Peter, **"Feed my lambs" (John 21:15).** Jesus apparently was conveying to Peter that he had an important role in taking care of young believers-- young in chronological age as well as young or early in their spiritual development. In addition, Peter needed to understand that humility is a requirement for working in Jesus' ministry.

Peter, Feed My Sheep.

Jesus asked Peter the question a second time with a slight variation. This time Jesus asked, **"Simon, son of Jonas, lovest thou me?"** (John 21:16). Notice that Jesus made no comparison between Peter's love of Him and his love for the fish. It is not difficult to love a human being more than one loves some fish. Peter certainly loves Jesus, the Son of God, more than he loves a few fishes— he had already said so. But perhaps, Jesus wanted Peter to do a self-examination to determine the extent to which he really loves Jesus. Did he love Jesus above everything in the world!

Peter needed to decide if he really loved Jesus more than he loved everyone and everything— unconditional and unwavering love! Would his love for Jesus be so passionate and spiritual that he would never, ever deny Jesus again? Peter responded, **"Yea, Lord; thou knowest that I love thee. He (Jesus) saith unto him, Feed my sheep" (John 15:16).** Was Jesus teaching Peter a lesson on humility, patience, and the need for assistance of the Holy Spirit?

Perhaps Peter needed to understand that some of the believers to whom he would minister would require his patience, persistency, and the assistance of the Holy Spirit. Regardless, Jesus told him to feed his sheep. Jesus had been the physical shepherd for the disciples for three years. Now Peter will assume the physical role. Peter will need to provide leadership in feeding the new converts as well as older—frail members of the Church. Jesus gives Peter an awesome assignment that Peter could not accomplish simply by his own volition. He would need to rely on the Holy Spirit, which he would receive on the day of Pentecost.

Jesus Requires Unconditional And Unwavering Love

Jesus asked Peter for the third time, **"Simon, son of Jonas, lovest thou me" (John 15:17).** By this time, Peter was perplexed because Jesus had asked the question three times. Could it be that Jesus wanted Peter to recall how he had denied Jesus three times when Jesus was being tried? When Peter denied Jesus, he was trying to save his own life, so three times, he denied ever knowing

Jesus. Evidently, Peter did not remember the teaching of Jesus, **"For whosoever shall save his life shall lose it: and whosoever shall lose his life for my sake shall find it" (Matthew 16:25; 10:39)**. Was Jesus asking Peter to make an unwavering, irreversible commitment to Him this time?

Peter Passes The Test Of Unconditional And Unwavering Love For Jesus

Jesus knew the heart of Peter. In addition, Jesus knew the challenges and tribulations which Peter would face as he carried out Jesus' assignment--Great Commission. Therefore, Jesus wanted Peter to prepare his heart and mind for his no turning back ministry. **"Jesus said unto him, Feed my sheep" (John 21:17).** Peter passed the test with flying colors. He knew that Jesus had indirectly chastised him, and he accepted the chastisement and the assignment.

Peter was grateful that Jesus forgave him and restored him to the important ministry of taking care of Jesus' lambs and sheep—His followers, young as well as mature—physically and spiritually. The Holy Spirit empowered Peter with boldness when he was converted on the Day of Pentecost--no more would he deny Jesus Christ.

Often, forgiveness is manifested in restoration. Jesus demonstrates to Peter, and just as importantly, to the other disciples, that Jesus forgives Peter for denying and restores Peter in fellowship with Jesus and with the rest of the disciples. Peter Jesus had an opportunity to testify on behalf of Jesus at Jesus' mock trial. Instead, he denied knowing Jesus. Jesus really did not need a human witness to testify for Him at His trial; because He has God. And the Prophets Isaiah and Zephaniah and Psalmists had already testified of Him. Nevertheless, Peter's testimony might have strengthened the other disciples at the time.

Peter compensated for his denial of Jesus and became one of the greatest apostles and advocates for Jesus Christ, the Messiah! This was possible because Jesus forgives and restores Peter. At Peter's first sermon on the Day of Pentecost, three thousand souls were converted (Acts 2:41).

The Power Of Forgiveness

The power of forgiveness is immense. In many cases, forgiveness benefits the person granting the forgiveness as much as it benefits the one forgiven. In the case of Jesus and Peter, Jesus retains a loyal apostle who would provide leadership in the early Church—it was on the true confession of Peter that Jesus is the Son of God that Jesus built the Church—and Peter was persistent and faithful in carrying out the Great Commission. Peter was relieved of the burden of guilt for betraying Jesus. In addition, he could now better understand and appreciate the lesson which Jesus had previously taught him and the other disciples on forgiving seventy times seven.

It is noteworthy that Jesus did not reprimand Peter for his unfaithfulness in denying Him; rather, Jesus strengthened Peter's resolve to be faithful to Jesus and restored him to fellowship with the other disciples and with Jesus Himself.

The Forgiven And Converted Peter Begins His Assignment

It is conceivable that when Peter preached on the Day of Pentecost, he thought of his act of cowardice in denying Jesus and how Jesus gave him a second chance. He allowed the Holy Spirit to take full control of him. He preached with boldness and supernatural power, overcompensating for his cowardice. Three thousand souls were converted. Perhaps, even some of the other apostles were converted as a result of the preaching of Peter. Jesus had previously told Peter, **"When thou art converted, strengthen thy brethren" (Luke 22:32).** And Peter did and was a spokesperson for the disciples during the early Church.

It all started as a result of the risen Jesus reaching out and forgiving Peter and restoring him to his leadership role among the other disciples. Yes, forgiveness is powerful, especially when it is accompanied by the restoration of the relationship. Jesus forgives Peter and forgot the hurt He felt when Peter denied knowing Him at his trial. But do not be too hard on Peter because he was not converted at the time, and the Spirit of Jesus was not dwelling in him at that time.

As a Christian believer, the Spirit of Jesus is dwelling in you. Are you willing and ready to forgive others as Jesus forgives Peter? Your answer should be yes. If you cannot answer with an affirmative yes, you need to ask God to help you forgive!

A Prayer For Your Forgiveness

I pray that you will be able to forgive those who have done you wrong, even when the wrong deeds are done maliciously. Further, I pray that you will forget the wrong and that you will restore relationship and fellowship with those you have forgiven, similarly to how Jesus Christ forgave Peter, forgot his denial, and restored relationship and fellowship with him. You and I are blessed through the ministry of the forgiven and converted Peter, who built on the foundation of the Church that Jesus Himself laid down. Yes, Jesus is the Door which leads into the Kingdom of God and forgiveness is the ticket or key to the Door! No one can enter through that door unless he or she forgives those who do wrong to him or her.

Chapter 7

Stephen: A Human Model Of Forgiveness

Speaking The Truth Boldly: Ready To Forgive And To Die

What would you request if you were being stoned to death and you have the ears of God – Jesus? What would you ask God – Jesus to do if you were being stoned to death because you were proclaiming the truth about Jesus Christ? What would you do or say if religious mobsters were stoning you and you knew that it was well with your soul?

We will see what Deacon Stephen did whilst he was stoned to death by an angry gang of self-righteous leaders and followers. We will pray that God will inspire our hearts to act appropriately when we are faced with difficulties, especially because of our proclamation of the Gospel. In a previous section of this book, I discussed the prayer of Stephen. In this section, I am focusing on the forgiveness of Stephen – his love at the time of his certain and imminent death.

The repentant dying criminal being crucified adjacent to Jesus asked Jesus to remember him when Jesus got into His Kingdom. Well, Deacon Stephen was being stoned shortly after the Day of Pentecost when three thousand persons, perhaps including Stephen, were converted.

Although he was 'just' a deacon – appointed by the apostles to take of the Grecian widows – the religious leaders at Jerusalem were offended and angered by his preaching. He had the audacity of preaching that Jesus was the Messiah, the Son of God and that the religious leaders had maliciously and vindictively murdered Him.

The Jewish religious leaders were envious of the character and work of Jesus and considered Him a threat to their misguided religious understanding and illegitimate religious authority. In addition, they were furious and annoyed when Stephen proclaimed that Jesus Christ, whom they murdered, rose from the dead and ascended into heaven.

Truly, Stephen's words were stunning to the adversaries of Jesus Christ. Stephen told them that they were stiff-necked and their hearts and ears were uncircumcised – they were not inclined to accept the truth. In addition, they were resisting the Holy Ghost as their fathers did. Then Stephen asked the heart-wrenching, rhetorical question, **"Which of the prophets have not your fathers persecuted?" (Acts 7:52).** Then Stephen placed the proverbial dagger in their ears and hearts when he told them that their fathers slew the prophets who predicted, **"The (the) coming of the Just One; of whom ye have been betrayers and murders" (Acts 7:52).** Stephen spoke the truth with clarity, boldness, and without apology. Certainly, he must have been aware of the consequences of speaking such truth so publicly and bluntly. Not only did Stephen accuse the fathers of the Jewish leaders of slaying prophets who foretold the coming of Jesus (such as Isaiah), but he accused the Jewish leaders of being betrayers and murderers of Jesus.

Truth Is Too Piercing To Accept: Murder The Messenger

While Stephen was speaking, the religious leaders and their followers were so angry that they gnashed their teeth at Deacon-Evangelist Stephen. **"But he, being full of the Holy Ghost looked up steadfastly into heaven, and saw the glory of God and Jesus standing on the right hand of God" (Acts 7:55).** God gave Stephen a glimpse of heaven. Stephen describes his supernatural experience in his own words, which he shouted out, **"Behold, I see the heavens opened, and the Son of man standing on the right hand of God" (Acts 7:56).** This proclamation was too much for the religious leaders to accept. These were the ones who crucified Jesus just a few months earlier. To them, Stephen had crossed the line of tolerance and respect for their misguided religion; he had to die.

The words of Deacon Stephen pierced the hearts of the religious leaders as a two-edged sword. While they were interrogating Stephen, they were boiling over with 'unrighteous' indignation. Before the interrogation was completed, they rushed upon Deacon Stephen, even before their certain false verdict was pronounced.

The religious leaders – high priests, Pharisees, Sadducees, scribes, elders-- and their Roman surrogates dragged Stephen out of the place of interrogation and out of the city limit. They had nothing but murder in their hearts and on their minds and their weapon of stones in their hands. And having given Saul (Paul) their outer garment to protect, they assailed Deacon Stephen with their weapon of murder – stones, envy, anger, and hatred. They wanted to see him dead. They did not understand that they could not kill the truth about Jesus by killing Stephen, a bearer of that truth.

Stephen Forgives His Executioners And Prays For Them

While the religious mob – executioners were stoning Stephen, God afforded Stephen a glimpse into the heavens, as stated above. Stephen knew that his death was imminent; however, he had the wonderful vision that Jesus was standing in heaven, at the right hand of God, waiting to welcome him to his permanent home. So,

Stephen did not ask God, Jesus, or the Holy Spirit to deliver him from the atrocity of the sincerely misguided and ignorant religious leaders and their followers. He did not ask God to send angels to protect him as God had done for Daniel in the lion's den or in the case of Shadrach, Meshach, and Abednego in the burning fiery furnace. He did not pronounce a curse upon the people who were stoning him. Rather, Stephen emulated Jesus Christ and cried out, asking God to forgive them.

Deacon Stephen knew that Jesus was the Door to the Kingdom of God, and he (Stephen) had the ticket to the Door. Not only Jesus was Jesus waiting to welcome Stephen – He standing, not sitting, eager to welcome Stephen to his heavenly home. Stephen was perfectly okay with his early transition into eternity; however, he was concerned with the fate of his transgressors.

So, Stephen knelt, and with every breath he had, and every strength he could muster, and with passion, the dying Stephen **"cried with a loud voice, Lord, lay not this sin to their charge" (Acts 7:60)**. Stephen, the first named martyr--follower of Jesus Christ--did not want his murders to be punished for violating God's Law which says," Thou **shall not kill" (Exodus 20:13)**. The high priests, Pharisees, scribes, elders and their followers were well familiar with the Law of Moses given by God, but that did not deter them from murdering the righteous Stephen.

Stephen Forgives Saul, An Accomplice To The Stoning

The young Pharisee Saul was well schooled in Jewish laws and customs, yet he consented to the murder of Stephen. But even so, Stephen did not wish for Saul to be punished for being an accomplice to his murder. Perhaps Stephen knew that Jesus had work for Saul to do. Stephen forgives all who were directly or indirectly involved in his murder by the cruelty of stoning, including Saul of Tarsus (Acts 7:58 – 60). Stephen asked God not to charge his murderers for their sins, including Saul. Evidently, Saul misunderstood the Scripture at the time and thought that he was doing God's work by murdering followers of Jesus. He thought that Jesus and His followers were fake blasphemers.

Stephen fully understood the consequences of speaking out for Jesus, and he was willing to accept the negative consequence of physical death for the positive reward of everlasting life. In addition, he was willing and delighted to forgive his murderers because he knew that vengeance belonged to God and all people belonged to God. It was the Spirit of Christ in Stephen which empowered him to forgive his murderers and to ask God to forgive them likewise. Such a miracle of forgiveness requires prayer. So Stephen asked God to forgive them after he had already forgiven them.

Are you willing to forgive someone who has done something egregious to you? It is difficult and perhaps impossibility for you to do so of your own volition. Such forgiveness is only possible when the Spirit of Jesus is in you. Jesus asks His disciples-us to do things that are impossible for natural persons to do on their own. Jesus once told the disciples, **"For it is easier for a camel to pass through the eye of a needle than for a rich man to enter the kingdom of God" (Luke 18:25).** The disciples were astonished at this teaching and exclaimed, **"Who then shall be saved?" (Luke 18:26).** At this point, Jesus calmly assures them, **"The things which are impossible**

with men are possible with God" (Luke 18:27). Jesus did not and does expect His disciples-followers to do humanly impossible things through their/our own volition, dedication, and effort alone. He expects us to work through the endowment of the Holy Spirit.

It was through the Holy Spirit working in Stephen which allowed Him to carry out Jesus' commandment, **"But I say unto you which hear, Love your enemies, do good to them which hate you. Bless them that curse you, and pray for them which despitefully use you" (Luke 6:27 – 28; Matthew 5:44).** It was not difficult for Stephen to carry out Jesus' commandment to love his enemies, to forgive them, and to pray for them because he was operating under the empowerment of the Holy Spirit.

Without God's Spirit in him, Stephen would not have been able to forgive those who were stoning him to death. Neither can followers of Jesus Christ do the humanly impossible things which Jesus asks us to do unless we are empowered by the Holy Spirit. This includes forgiving those who have abused and or are abusing us.

Sometimes Christians – believers find it impossible and, at best difficult to forgive. Often it is because they are trying to forgive by their own volition and effort. The desire to forgive is a good first step; however, truly forgiving someone for egregious atrocities requires the help of the Holy Spirit. Luke records, **"And Stephen, full of faith and power, did great wonders and miracles among the people" (Acts 6:8).** Clearly, in order to truly forgive another, one has to have faith in God and the empowerment of the Holy Spirit. So, if you have the desire to forgive someone and you are having difficulty in doing so, go to Go in sincere prayer and ask for His assistance. Bear in mind that you will need the empowerment of the Holy Spirit. The good news is that you receive the Holy Spirit the moment you accept Jesus Christ as your Lord and Savior. Only when you are empowered by the Holy Spirit are you able to forgive as Stephen did. And only when you, as a believer, forgive others can you expect God to forgive you. Remember, forgiveness is quintessential for entering the Kingdom of God. It is my prayer that you will strive to have the desire and reality to forgive as Stephen.

Chapter 8

The Risen Jesus Forgives Saul

Saul, The Persecutor, Consents To The Stoning Of Stephen

Paul was a well-educated Jew, a Pharisee, and a citizen of Judah and Rome. He originated from Tarsus, a city in Cilicia – a Roman Province, and was of pure Jewish descent, of the tribe of Benjamin. He migrated to Jerusalem to study under the great Rabbi Gamaliel – a teacher of the (Jewish) Law (acts 22:3).

Saul (Jewish name) first came into recognition at the stoning of Deacon Stephen – the first recorded martyr of the followers of Jesus. Saul consented to the stoning of Stephen – in fact, he aided and abetted in the stoning of Stephen by securing the outer coats of those who were stoning Stephen and watching them stoned Stephen to death.

Luke records, "And Stephen, full of faith and power, did great wonders and miracles among the people" (Acts 6:8). Many educated people disputed with Stephen in the synagogue – perhaps, including Saul since people from Cilicia, Saul's hometown, were among those who argued against the Gospel Stephen was preaching. They could not successfully counter the Gospel, so they decided to kill Stephen. (Acts 6:8 – 15; 7:51 – 60). For further details on the incident, see Chapter 7 of this book – Stephen: The Human Model of Forgiveness.

Paul Confesses His Involvement In Persecutions And Murders

Stephen was not the first follower of Jesus, who Saul assisted in murdering. When Paul was arrested in the Temple at Jerusalem, after his Damascus experience and his conversion, for preaching that Jesus is the Messiah, he confessed that he was involved in other persecutions and murders prior to the stoning of Stephen.

As a Roman captain and Roman soldiers were leading Paul into the barracks at Jerusalem to prevent the Jews from killing him, the Roman captain granted him permission to address the crowd. Paul identified himself as a Jew, born in Tarsus, a city of Cilicia, who had studied under the great Rabbi Gamaliel at Jerusalem.

Then Paul confessed, **"And I persecuted this way unto the death, binding and delivering into prisons both men and women. As also the high priest doth bear me witness, and all the estate (council) of the elders: from whom also I received letters (to persecute followers of Jesus at Damascus)" (Acts 22:4 – 5).** Paul persecuted followers of Jesus and even in murders with the full authorization and support of the Jewish religious leaders. But when he encountered the risen Jesus on his way to Damascus to persecute followers of Jesus, he became a new man and could no longer persecute followers of Jesus.

Paul was now being persecuted by the Jewish religious leaders for preaching that Jesus is the Messiah – delivering the same message for which he had persecuted the followers of Jesus – and for which the Jewish religion was persecuting him and sought to kill him. He was reaping what he had sown, as Jesus had revealed to the Disciple Ananias, who ministered to Saul at Damascus and restored his sight. In fact, before his confession, at Jerusalem, he wrote to the Galatian believers in approximately A. D. 49, **"Be not deceived; God has not mocked: for whatsoever a man soweth, that shall he also reap" (Galatians 6:7)**. By the time he wrote to the Galatian believers, he was already experiencing persecution by the Jewish religious leaders, and they considered him a traitor for preaching the truth about Jesus.

But how was Saul changed from a persecutor of followers of Jesus to an advocate for Jesus to the extent that he was being persecuted? His Damascus experiences explain his transformation. It is important to remember that the foregoing incident occurred years after Saul's Damascus experiences – after his conversion. I will now resume Saul's Damascus experience.

Saul's Damascus Experiences: Conversion And Transformation

After the stoning of Stephen, Saul was emboldened by his persecution of the followers of Jesus. He went to the high priest and obtained a letter authoring him to go to Damascus and arrest and take to Jerusalem in chains, anyone – men or women--he found preaching/teaching about Jesus. Saul and his enforcers went on their journey with the letter of authorization to arrest and take followers of Jesus to Jerusalem. They had no notion that the risen Jesus was observing everything. After all, they had gotten away with murdering Stephen – so they thought. So on the outskirt of Damascus 'out of nowhere – out of heaven came a light which struck them to the ground.

The risen Jesus revealed Himself to Saul and sent him to Damascus to receive instructions from a disciple, Ananias. It is quite likely that Ananias was a disciple that Saul intended to arrest and take back to Jerusalem in chains. Saul obeyed Jesus and went to Damascus in search of Ananias.

Jesus Forgives Saul For Persecuting-Murdering His Followers

Saul was in Damascus for three days without sight. Jesus sent Ananias, a disciple residing in Damascus, to minister to Saul. Ananias ministered to him, and he was converted – from a well-educated Jewish religious persecutor of followers to a devoted advocate of Jesus Christ of Nazareth, the Son of God.

Jesus forgives Saul for his heinous crimes against His disciples. And gives him a special assignment – as a chosen vessel to preach to the Gentiles and to witness before kings and the children of Israel. But Jesus did not exonerate Saul of all consequences of his evil deeds prior to his conversion. In fact, Jesus reveals to Ananias, **"For I will shew him how great things he must suffer for my name's sake" (Acts 9:16).**

Saul was well physically and intellectually prepared for the assignment. Besides, Saul was totally committed and sincere persuasive, and persistent in his endeavors. Yes, he prepared for his special assignment – And Jesus endowed him with the power of the Holy Spirit when Ananias laid his hand on him. As previously stated, he was well educated. He was a Jew and Pharisee and a citizen of Judah and of Rome.

The Apostle Paul, as he referred to himself after his conversion – probably wanted to symbolize that he was a new creation – became one of the most dedicated advocates of Jesus Christi – preaching and spreading the Gospel-the good news. He arguably was the most effective evangelist in the Bible. He was one of the most eloquent writers – writing thirteen or fourteen epistles and planting more churches than anyone else recorded in the Bible.

All this and more happened because Jesus Christ forgave Saul for his misunderstandings and crimes and gave him a special assignment, and empowered him with the Holy Spirit to carry out the assignment.

Jesus will do the same for you. But are you willing to forgive others for their egregious crimes against you, or your loved ones are against society? Are you hurting as a result of injustices toward you or toward others you care about? On your own, it might be impossible for you to forgive some 'unforgivable.' But Jesus said, **"The things which are impossible with men are possible with God" (Luke 18:27).** Jesus requires many seemingly impossible things of His followers – for which forgiving, in some situations, might be one – and they might indeed be impossible if the followers try to do them on their own volition and determination alone.

However, Jesus expects us to pray and seek the empowerment of the Holy Spirit. He stated that expectation in this manner, **"And he spake a parable unto them to this end, that men ought always to pray, and not to faint" (Luke 18:1).** It is important to involve God in your forgiving process because there might be instances which require divine intervention in order for you to forgive.

In addition, Jesus told His disciples that some miracles require prayer and fasting, such as when He cast the evil spirit out of the father's son (Matthew 17:21; Mark 9:29). Certainly, some forgiveness requires a miracle, which you can ask God to perform for you through your prayers and fasting. So cultivate the desire to forgive and pray earnestly, sincerely, and continuously with the confident expectation that God will answer your prayer. And God will help you to forgive.

Our unforgiveness will block the entrance to the Gate, leading to eternal life. So let us forgive!

Chapter 9

Paul's Teachings About Forgiveness

Forgive As God Forgives You For Christ's Sake

The Apostle Paul had every reason to forgive others and to urge, in fact, admonish believers to forgive others. After all, Saul (Paul), the learned Pharisee, a Jew, and a Roman citizen, aided and abetted in the malicious murder of Deacon Stephen. In addition, the converted Saul (Paul) confessed that he was involved in the murder of others – both men and women--believers in Jesus prior to the murder of Stephen (Acts 22:4). Saul, who was an enforcer of the Jewish Law – the Law of Moses, **"Thou shalt not kill" (Exodus 20:13),** was guilty of breaking that Law.

No one doubted the converted Saul, who now used his Roman name Paul was extremely grateful that Jesus had forgiven him for his murders and persecutions. So in his Epistle to perhaps his most loved church congregation at Ephesus, he admonishes believers to forgive one another. Paul writes from Rome, where he is essentially under house arrest, **"And be ye kind to one another, tenderhearted, forgiving one another, even as God for Christ's sake hath forgiven you" (Ephesians 4:32).** It is significant that Paul mentions that God has forgiven the Ephesian believers for Christ's sake.

Paul (formerly Saul) persecuted and aided, and abetted the murder of believers in Jesus Christ. And is now in prison (house arrest) for preaching about the same Jesus whose followers he once persecuted. Paul wanted the Ephesian believers to remember or understand that Jesus paid a heavy price for their forgiveness – He gave up His life on Calvary's Cross so that God was able to forgive them. So since God forgives the Ephesian believers because Christ paid the price for their forgiveness, they should be willing to forgive others regardless of the infractions against them – no infraction can be compared to the righteous Son of God laying down His life that God might forgive those – including the Ephesian believers who transgress against God.

Not only did God forgive Saul for persecuting followers of Jesus and for murdering women and men;

rather, Jesus gave Paul a special assignment – Commission to minister to Gentiles and Jews and to preach the Gospel to kings. Paul was truly grateful and understood the importance of forgiveness.

As a Christian and a believer in Jesus, you must be willing to forgive others, and you must encourage others to forgive when the opportunity presents itself. Remember that forgiveness is the key that opens the Door through which you enter the Kingdom of God.

It is intuitive to believe that at the time Paul was admonishing the Ephesian believers to forgive one another, he had already forgiven those who were responsible for him to be under house arrest in Rome – this was all a part of Jesus' plan for Paul to preach the Gospel in Rome.

By the time Paul was experiencing his house imprisonment in Rome, he had already written to the Romans, **"And we know that all things worketh for good to them that love God, to them who are the called according to the purpose of God" (Romans 8:28).** You might be going through a challenging situation – difficult to forgive; however, when you place your trust in God, He will assist you in working things out to your benefit. As Paul reminded the Ephesian believers, consider what Jesus did to make it possible for God to forgive you. It is very unlikely that you will need to give up your life in order to forgive someone. However, you might need to give the situation to God, who is able to handle it to your satisfaction. Things which are impossible with men are possible with God (Luke 18:27).

Forbearing One Another And Forgiving, Even As Christ Forgave You

While the time was under house arrest (Imprisonment in Rome), as previously discussed, he wrote to the Colossian believers at the Church at Colosse'. The Epistle to the Colossian believers is remarkably similar to the one to the Ephesian believers. Again, Paul addresses the subject of forgiveness and other matters. Regarding the infractions against the Colossian believers, Paul admonishes them; **"Put on therefore, as elect of God, holy and beloved, bowels of mercies, kindness, humbleness of mind, meekness, longsuffering; Forbearing one another, and forgiving**

one another, if any man has a quarrel against any: even as Christ forgave you, so also do ye" (Colossians 3:12 – 13). The previous commentary on Paul's gratefulness for God's forgiveness is applicable in his Epistles to the Colossians as well.

Paul makes the case that Colossian believers should demonstrate the Christian qualities cited above. One of the acts of the elect of God – a believer in Jesus Christ – is not to be judgmental of others' faults; instead, forgive one another to a similar extent to how Christ forgave them. Certainly, Christ paid the ultimate price for the forgiveness of believers – He gave up His life. This suggests that there might be a great cost associated with forgiving others. However, Christ has already paid the high cost. Therefore believers are able to turn to Jesus for assistance in forgiving others, especially when such forgiveness seems impossible.

The urging of Paul to the Colossian believers to forgive one another is an example that believers of our times should emulate. You must forgive because you need God's forgiveness in order to enter the Kingdom of God. Because all – you and I--have sinned and come short of the glory of God. And the wages of sin is death (Romans 3:23; 6:23). As a believer, as stated previously, you have a moral and spiritual obligation to encourage believers to forgive others. Perhaps this book has helped you to forgive others, and you are now able to encourage others to forgive, based on the teaching of Jesus, Paul and others, and more importantly, based on your own experience of forgiving someone or some others.

John Mark Deserted Barnabas And Paul

While Paul and Barnabas were ministering in a highly successful Church at Antioch in Syria, the Holy Spirit told the church leadership to allow Paul and Barnabas to go on an evangelism journey. The Church harkened to the instruction of the Holy Spirit and, after praying for Paul and Barnabas and laying hands on them – blessing them--sent them off on their First Missionary Journey.

Along the way, Barnabas and Paul arrived at Seleucia, where John Mark (a Cousin of Barnabas) joined Barnabas and Paul on the Missionary Journey. However, when the evangelist reached Perga in Pamphylia, John

Mark abandoned the journey and returned to Jerusalem. Evidently, John Mark's behavior did not go well with Paul's (Acts 13:5, 13). Barnabas and Paul completed the journey and returned to Antioch.

Paul Refuses To Take John Mark On His Second Missionary Journey

After Barnabas and Paul had been at the Church at Antioch for some time after the First Missionary Journey, Paul suggested to Barnaba that they should go on a Second Missionary Journey. Barnabas quickly agreed with Paul and wanted his cousin John Mark to accompany them on that journey. However, Paul objected because John Mark deserted them on the First Missionary Journey and Paul was concerned that he would do that again. Paul's disagreement was so strong that he and Barnabas agreed to separate and go on their own journey. Barnabas took John Mark, and Paul took Silas.

Paul Chastisement Of John Mark Works Out Well

For many years, I have thought that Paul was tough on John Mark for not being kinder to him and giving him a second chance to accompany him and Barnabas on their Second Missionary Journey. Only after I wrote the paragraph above it occurred to me that Paul might have been sending an invaluable message to John Mark regarding the importance of commitment and loyalty. John Mark demonstrated a lack of commitment and loyalty when he deserted Barnabas and Paul at Perga in Pamphylia during the First Missionary Journey.

John Mark would need to be committed and loyal to Jesus to be a valuable follower and apostle of Jesus. So John Mark might have learned a lesson from Paul, which helped to make him a better evangelist and a reliable follower of Jesus.

Paul was sincere and committed even when he was a misguided persecutor of followers of Jesus. And no doubt, Paul demanded commitment and sincerity from his colleagues. John Mark got the message and benefited from it, as discussed below.

The chastisement of John Mark and his subsequent forgiveness suggests that, at least in some instances, chastisement might precede forgiveness. This brings to mind the admonishment of one writer of Proverbs, **"He that spareth his rod hateth his son: but he that loveth him chasteneth him betimes. (Proverb13:24).** There is no doubt that Paul considered John Mark as a spiritual son, even though he needed correction at the time of the start of Paul's Secondary Missionary Journey.

In addition, Paul was certainly aware of another admonition in Proverbs, **"Chasten thy son while there is hope, and let not thy soul spare for his crying" (Proverbs 19:18).** Paul waited for the appropriate time – when John Mark wanted to accompany him on his Second Missionary Journey – to chastise him. Paul exercised the appropriate chastisement, which undoubtedly had a tremendously positive and lasting impact on John Mark, even though John Mark might not have realized it at the time

Paul Forgives John Mark And Reconciles With Him

There is no doubt that Paul was furious with John Mark. But it is not clear at one point he forgave him. However, it is clear that Paul did forgive John Mark. During his second imprisonment in Rome – real imprisonment – no house arrest, he wrote to Timothy, **"Only Luke is with me. Take (John) Mark, and bring him with thee: for he is profitable to me for the ministry" (2 Timothy 4:11)**. Not only did Paul forgave Mark for deserting him on his First Missionary Journey, but evidently he had a special assignment for John Mark. Paul was in prison, and John Mark would help in his ministry. Forgiveness can have great power for the forgiver and the forgiven.

In the Epistle of Colossians, Paul mentions that John Mark was with him and sent greetings to the believers at Colossae. In addition, Paul asked the Colossian believers to welcome John Mark if he was in their midst (Colossians 4:10). Paul forgave John Mark and gave him a second chance, and John Mark became an invaluable asset to Paul and to the Gospel of Christ. He is the same John Mark who is generally credited for being the first writer of a Gospel: The Gospel According to Mark. Forgiveness suggests second, third, and fourth chances. In fact, Jesus told Peter that he must forgive not seven times; rather seven times seventy times – as many times as the perpetrator seeks forgiveness.

Paul Forgives His Deserters At His Trial In Rome

There is an old adage: *a friend in need is a friend indeed.* Evidently, Paul had some fair-weather friends or companions when he was in prison in Rome. They were with him when things were tolerable. However, when his long-awaited trial started, the less than faithful companions deserted Paul. This brings to mind the trial of Jesus when His disciples deserted Him, and Peter, who was in the back of the courtroom, denied that he even knew Jesus. Both Jesus and Paul had fair weather companions – when the going got tough, fair weather friends copped out.

Paul lamented that only Luke was with him (2 Timothy 4:11). Then Paul expressed such disappointment, **"At my first answer (trial) no man stood with me, but all men forsook me: I pray God that**

it may not be laid to their charge" (2 Timothy 4:16). When Paul defended himself against false charges all his companions deserted him – probably trying to protect themselves from similar charges. So similar to the fake trial of Jesus.

When I read Paul's statement that all men deserted him, it broke my heart. I could hardly fight back the tears. I am a huge admirer of Paul even though I have not met him in the flesh. I wondered how his friends could have treated him in that manner. However, I took comfort in Paul's forgiveness of his deserters.

As in the case of Stephen, who prayed for those who were stoning him, to whose stoning Paul (Saul) had consented – aided and abetted, Paul prayed for his deserters as Stephen had prayed for his murderers. Paul prays, **"I pray God that it may not be laid to their charge" (2 Timothy 4:16).** You can feel the hurt in Paul when he looks around and sees none of his companions, perhaps with the exception of the Gentile, Dr. Luke. Yet as in the incident with Stephen, which is discussed in Chapter 7 of this book, Paul forgives his companions who deserted him and prays for them.

Have you ever been deserted or abandoned by someone you trusted who might have been able to assist you in a dire situation? If so, have you been able to forgive that person and even pray for him or her that God would forgive him or her? Such forgiveness of others by the believer is possible because the Spirit of Jesus is present in the believer.

The Apostle Paul was quite familiar with the teaching of Jesus that not only should he forgive his deserters. Rather, he must **"But I say unto you, Love your enemies, bless them that curse you, do good to them that hate you, and pray for them which despitefully use you, and persecute you" (Matthew 5:44).** Paul had done exactly what Jesus instructs His followers to do – forgive and pray even for the enemies. However, it should not go unnoticed that although Jesus forgives Saul (Paul) for his atrocities against His followers

Paul was not exonerated from all consequences of his past behaviors – persecutions and murders of followers of Jesus. Nevertheless, Paul accepted his chastisement gracefully and was ready to forgive. Prior to his imprisonment in Rome, Paul asserted to the Philippian believers. "I can do all things through Christ which strengtheneth me" (Philippians 4:13). Paul's ability to forgive was rooted in Christ living in him.

As a believer, you can learn much from Paul. He took the teaching of Jesus seriously and was able to forgive those who essentially denied or even betrayed him. With the Spirit of Jesus in you, you are able to forgive even the seemingly unforgivable. Because things which are impossible with men are possible with God. And since God is in you, forgiving others is possible with you as well.

Paul Admonishes Colossian Christians To Forgive

The Apostle Paul was in prison in Rome when he wrote his amazing letter to Christians in the Church at Colosse. Paul had learned of the faith of the saints- Christians in Jesus Christ and their love for one another. He wanted to encourage them and let them know that he was continuously praying for them. (Colossians 1:1 – 4). Paul gave great exhortations and encouragement to those

Christians. He urges them to demonstrate godly qualities such as compassion, kindness, humbleness of mind, meekness, and patience (Colossians (3:12). ThenPaul addresses the need for forgiveness. He puts it this way, **"Forbearing (be tolerant of) one another, and forgiving one another, if any man have a quarrel against any: even as Christ forgave you, so also do ye" (Colossians 3:13).** Here, Paul instructs the Colossians that forgiveness is not an option; rather forgiveness is an expectation of all Christians.

Paul's instruction to the Colossian Christians-believers is applicable to believers of our time. Forgiving others for their wrongs is not optional for believers; however, the sincere forgiveness that Paul, in fact, Jesus, demands is only possible when the Spirit of Jesus/God dwells in the believers. True believers possess the Spirit of Jesus/God to render true and unconditional forgiveness even to those who seem 'unforgivable.' In fact, it is the Christ in the Christian believer who makes it possible to totally forgive. Paul simply emphasizes the teaching of Jesus, **"For if ye (we) forgive men their trespasses, your heavenly father will also forgive you (us)" (Matthew 6:14).**

Chapter 10

Lord, Please, Help Me To Forgive

Struggling With Forgiving: Turn It Over To God

Some Miracles Require Prayer and Fasting

A father took his demon-possessed son to Jesus for healing. When the man arrived, Jesus and three of His disciples – Peter, James, and John--had gone to the Mount of Transfiguration. The other disciples could not heal the young man. When Jesus returned to the place where the other disciples were, He found the disappointed and agitated father with his demon-possessed son. The father explained his situation to Jesus and expressed his disappointment that the disciples could not heal his son.

Jesus understood the pain and disappointment of this distressed father. Jesus had compassion for the man and his son. He rebuked the evil spirit and cast it out of the young man. He ordered the evil spirit not to enter the young man anymore.

When Jesus and His disciples got into a house, the disciples asked Jesus why they were unable to cast the evil spirit out of the young man. Jesus answered them, **"Howbeit this kind (of evil spirit) goeth not but by prayer and fasting" (Matthew 17:21; Mark 9:29).** I have included this incident to suggest that sometimes forgiveness – our totally and fully forgiving others – requires a miracle. And the miracle requires prayer and fasting.

It is the Spirit of God in you who makes it possible for you to forgive heinous atrocity against you. Paul puts such ability to forgive in this manner, **"For it is God which worketh in you both to will and to do of his good pleasure" (Philippians 2:13).** As good as your intention might be, you cannot forgive certain wrongs simply by your own volition. But with the assistance of the Spirit of God/Jesus in you, it is possible for you to say as Paul says, **"I can do all things through Christ which strengtheneth me" (Philippians 4:13).** Yes, God shows up with a miracle when you really need one. On this, you can depend and trust God.

You might be so overwhelmed by the atrocity against you that you cannot even think about forgiveness. You are a human being, and you might be experiencing righteous indignation. Someone has violated you so badly that you are filled with anger, and all you can think of for a while is revenge – the perpetrator-offender must pay – you are thinking. You want justice.

Certainly, your feeling is understandable from a human and natural person perspective. However, you are familiar with many passages in the Bible which speak out to you and me on how we should handle infractions of others against us. I list a few.

Dealing With Infractions And Atrocities

God, Himself said, **"To me (Him) belongeth vengeance, and recompence; their foot shall slide at due time" (Deuteronomy 32:35).** Here, God is saying to leave things in His hands, and He will handle your hurt and pains and deal with your offender. And Jesus instructs His followers**, "Ye have heard that it hath been said, AN EYE FOR AN EYE, AND A TOOTH FOR**

A TOOTH: But I say unto you, That ye resist not evil: but whosoever shall smite thee on the right cheek, turn unto him the other also" (Matthew 5:38 – 39). You probably say to yourself that this instruction of Jesus might have been doable when Jesus walked amongst men. But things are quite different now. People have little respect for others, and many have no conscience – they will hurt others and don't even think about what they do for a second.

The Apostle Paul admonishes **Roman believers and us, "Dearly beloved, avenge not yourselves, but rather give place unto wrath: for it is written, VENGEANCE IS MINE, I WILL REPAY, saith the Lord. Be not overcome of evil, but overcome evil with good" (Romans 12:19-21).** You may ask the legitimate questions: Are the instructions and admonitions cited above relevant to you today, and is it really possible to carry out those seemingly impossible instructions? Whichever answer you choose, you are correct. The instructions are applicable and relevant to believers of our times, but the natural human being cannot carry out the instructions of his or her own volition – so the answer to both questions is yes. However, only the transformed human being filled with the Holy Spirit – the born-again believer is able to carry out the instructions.

There should be no pretension that it is easy to carry out the instructions to forgive, especially the seemingly 'unforgivable' offenders – such forgiveness requires a miracle that comes about by your love, your faith, and God's grace. Remember that forgiving someone for an egregious crime against you might very well be the greatest test of your true love and unwavering faith. This might indeed require a miracle.

Think about it. As I stated previously, it is not because a person has sinned that will prevent that person from receiving eternal life. Rather, it is the refusal of that person to forgive others so that he or she may seek God's forgiveness. Again, I am referring to the person who is a believer. So if it is difficult for the believer to forgive at times, then certainly a miracle – work of the Holy Spirit – is essential for true forgiveness seventy times seven – at all times.

Love And Forgive

Sometimes it is really difficult to forgive. But the good news is that as a true believer--born-again saint, you have the Spirit of Jesus in you urging you to forgive. I want to reiterate that some hurt, pains, injuries, and atrocities are much too heinous for you to forgive of your own volition. So you must submit your natural self to the Holy Spirit – the Spirit of Jesus in you. As I said above, it is God who will carry out the miracle. For you to forgive requires two decisions on your part – I am only speaking to you who have accepted Jesus Christ as your Lord and Savior – not to the not-yet Christian believer – I will speak with that person a little later.

Firstly, you must have a genuine desire to forgive, and you do have a consequential reason for wanting to forgive – your eternal life is at stake, at risk. Therefore your desire to forgive should be strong and unwavering. You must forgive others if you want God to forgive you. I will repeat a quote of Jesus regarding forgiveness, **"And when ye stand praying, forgive, if ye have ought against any: that your Father which is in heaven forgive you your trespasses" (Mark 11:25).** As I stated previously in this book, Paul reminds us that we have all sinned and fell short of God's expectation of us. Therefore, you and I need God's forgiveness.

Matthew records Jesus' admonition in this manner, **"For if ye forgive men their trespasses, your heavenly Father will also forgive you" (Matthew 6:14)**. Jesus makes it very clear that God will forgive you if you forgive those who have done you wrong. Remember that I am speaking with you who have already accepted Jesus Christ as your Savior. Only those who have accepted Jesus Christ as Savior are in a position to refer to God as "Our Father." So, clearly, Jesus is referring to Christians-believers to forgive others before seeking God's forgiveness for themselves.

Because the love of Jesus is in you – even though you have slipped and fallen short of God's expectation – you will want to keep and strive to keep the two great Commandments, **"THOU SHALT LOVE THE LORD THY GOD WITH ALL THY HEART, AND WITH ALL THY SOUL, AND WITH ALL THY MIND, This is the first and great commandment. And the second is like unto it, THOUGH SHALT LOVE THY**

NEIGHBOUR AS THYSELF" (Matthew 22:37 – 39). It is important to remember that when the love of Jesus is in your heart, you want the best for your neighbor, even when he or she hurts you. You should want your neighbor to repent and accept Jesus as his or her Savior. The converted neighbor will be your brother or sister in Christ. You will be joyful!

It is not only by your own volition which gives you the desire to forgive. Rather, it is the love of Jesus in you that makes you want the best for your brothers or sisters, even your enemies who hurt you. So it is not just about you. Rather, it is about Jesus and what He has done to win your pardon and forgiveness and that of your brothers and sisters. So love and forgiveness go hand in hand for the believer in Jesus Christ. Jesus admonishes His followers, **"Love your enemies, bless them that curse you, do good for them that hate you, and pray for them that despitefully use you, and persecute you" (Matthew 5:44).** Where there is love, there is the desire to forgive. You cannot truly forgive someone until you truly love him or her. And remember that Jesus teaches that loving your neighbor is the second greatest commandment – second only to loving God.

Secondly, after having a genuine desire to forgive, you must believe that God is able to assist you in forgiving the perpetrator(s) for his or her or their heinous crime(s), infraction(s), and or atrocities against you. In addition, you must believe that God will assist you when you seek His assistance. It is very important that you believe that God will help you deal with your physical and emotional pains and will help you to forgive. However, more importantly, He will forgive your transgressions against Him when you seek His forgiveness.

Receiving God's Because God's forgiveness is necessary for you to have eternal life. So forgiving others is really a big deal. It is conceivable that your hurting might be so bad – physically and emotionally that you are not thinking about eternal life at the time. Rather, your mind is probably focused on wanting justice or something that will ease your pains-your hurt, even revenge. Well, Jesus is feeling your pains and your hurt as well, and He is ready to assist you as no other can. But you must ask God's help in the name of Jesus. Yes, it's easier said than done, but you can do it because the Spirit of Jesus is in you. And Jesus is eager to help you.

Believing In God Results In Miracles

Because you believe in Jesus, you are likely familiar with the 'Faith' Epistle, Hebrews. The writer of Hebrew reminds you and me, **"But without faith it is impossible to please him (God): for he that cometh to God must believe that he is, and that he is a rewrder of them that diligently seek him" (Hebrews 11:6).** You believe that God is who He says He is and that He is able to do what He promises He will do And that He will do what He promises. Therefore, you must collaborate with Him in doing tasks He asks you to do – to let Him help you forgive.

Believing that God will do what He promises is very important. The Bible reminds us that Abraham believed God's Promise to him, **"And he (Abraham) believed in the LORD; and he (God) counted it to him (Abraham) for righteous" Genesis 15:6.** An essential component of being able to forgive is believing that God will help you to forgive. When you believe God, He counts or considers you righteous – you already believe in God – God looks out for His righteous people.

Daniel believed in God, and God rewarded him with a great miracle – God shut the lions' mouths so that they could not hurt Daniel. The malicious Babylonians threw him in the lions' den, and God sent angels to protect Daniel. The Bible records, **"So Daniel was taken up out of the den, and no manner of hurt was found upon him, because he believed in his God" (Daniel 6:23)**. Certainly, the God who saved Daniel from the hungry lions is able to help you forgive, you only need to believe as Daniel did.

You are now convinced that God will assist you to forgive; nevertheless, I share one of God's declarations regarding His power to do whatever He wants--including giving you the miracle to help you forgive. When the people of Judah were in captivity in Babylon, God instructed Jeremiah to buy fields in Judah. Jeremiah was a little hesitant to buy fields in Judah at the time Babylonians were occupying Jerusalem-Judah. But God's admonition to Jeremiah was succinct and clear, **"Behold, I am the LORG, the God of all flesh: is there anything too hard for me?" (Jeremiah 32:27).** That was a rhetorical question to Jeremiah.

Of course, there is nothing too hard for God. God had already made plans to deliver the people of Judah at His appointed time. Surely, God will assist you to forgive and will create a forgiving heart in you to match your love for God and for your neighbor – and even your enemy – you need only to ask God in the name of Jesus and believe!

Love Precedes Forgiveness

And remember, Jesus is your advocate and mediator, sitting at the right hand of God, advocating on your behalf. Besides, the Spirit of Jesus – Holy Spirit-- is in you, empowering you to show your love for God and for your neighbor-offender-- through your forgiveness.

For the natural person, forgiving someone for the type of infractions you have endured would be impossible. But with God working in you and through you, it is possible for you to forgive the worst of infractions – and not really you forgiving, but God working on your behalf. To repeat, this type of forgiveness requires prayer and may require meditation and fasting as well. Forgiving others is not an option for you; rather, it is a quintessential requirement for eternal life. So the more difficult it is for you to forgive a person or persons, the more time you must spend with God, praying in the name of Jesus with confident expectation that He will answer your prayer.

You Cannot Truly Forgive A Person Who You Do Not Truly Love

Remember, you cannot truly forgive a person who you do not truly love – agape' (spiritual) love. When you find it difficult to forgive someone, search your heart and determine whether you feel love in your heart for that person. If you do not feel agape' for that person, you must ask God to open your heart so that you are able to love that person. Not hating a person or not having anything against a person may be a feeling of indifference and is not the same as loving the person spiritually – agape'. Again, love, faith, and forgiveness go hand in hand. When the love of Jesus Christ is in your heart, you will love others.

If you are a believer-born-again, you are sure to have the mind of Jesus in you. The Apostle Paul reminds us, **"Let this mind be in you, which was also in Christ Jesus" (Philippians 2:5)**. This was a mind of love, obedience, humility, holiness, concern-considerate, patience, godliness, forgiving, fellowship with and delight in God, and so forth. There is no question regarding the extent to which Jesus Christ went to earn forgiveness for humanity. You and I have an obligation to forgive others and to bring them in fellowship with Jesus Christ. Because of the love of Jesus Christ, which is shed abroad in our hearts through the Holy Spirit.

The love of Jesus Christ is in your heart. You have the desire to forgive, and you have the faith that God is able to assist you in forgiving. So ask God to forgive, and have a confident expectation that He will assist you to forgive.

Chapter 11

Personal Experiences With Forgiveness

Targeted For Speaking The Truth

I consider myself blessed and extremely fortunate that only on one occasion in my forty years of employment at multiple agencies and institutions was I specifically targeted for unjust treatment. In his case, my employer wanted to get rid of me because I dared to raise questions regarding an unwise and perhaps ethically questionable decision the organization was making. I voiced my opinion on the matter. I was not invited to participate in any further discussions on the subject.

A few months after I had raised questions and expressed my opinion during a meeting, my employment contract for the upcoming year was changed from a regular annual contract to a month-by-month letter of employment. The administration surely knew that I would not accept the month-by-month letter of employment. It wanted me to leave but had no basis on which it could legitimately fire-dismiss me. I left about three months after receiving the unacceptable letter of employment. By the way, I learned later that the funding agency, in its audit of the organization program, raised the questions which I had raised.

As you might agree, I thought that I had good reasons to retaliate, even to contact the funding agency. However, I could not see myself doing anything that would hurt the organization. I had a decision to make – forgive and move on--or maintain unforgiveness and bitterness. I chose to forgive and move on. After all, I was and am a practicing Christian – and believe the teaching of the Apostle Paul, **"And we know that all things work together for the good to them that love God, to them who are the called according to his purpose" (Romans 8:28).** At the time of the incident described above, I might have wondered what good I could expect.

Well, I retired from employment. I went home and started to pray and meditate, and what would you know? I started to write. And you are now enjoying my fourth book in three years – and I have another manuscript that will be published soon and another manuscript that is almost completed.

In addition to the spiritual inspiration I receive, I am inspired by a quote attributed to Dean Martin, "The best revenge is massive success." I don't claim to have achieved massive success; however, the books which I have written and am writing are inspirational and are impacting lives in America and in other countries. My decision as a Christian to forgive and move on was based on my belief that God has a bigger purpose for me, and I have been working on that bigger purpose since I left that organization.

The decision to forgive and move on was affirmed by what I read two years later, *"God can miraculously turn the wrong decisions of others to work for your good"* (Mike Murdock, The Assignment). God certainly has given me a larger and more important assignment than I had with the organization.

I forgive the three persons at the organization who were responsible for my leaving. And I am so thankful to God and to them; because all things are working together for my good and for the good of people around the world who are benefitting from the books. Interestingly, I was energized when I left that organization and more determined to touch significantly more lives than the number I was working hard to assist when I was employed at the organization. All things taken together do work for the good of those who love God and respond to God's guidance.

Egregious And Inhumane Treatment Based On Prejudice, But Forgive: The Man With The Broken Car

Don't help him; let him go somewhere else: he almost lost his cool.

His small, almost tiny MGB car broke down in the heat of hot summer noonday in a Southwest Mississippi town. He was taking his five-year-old daughter to town and had traveled 23 miles and was almost in the town.

He lifted his daughter in his arms and walked about one-eighth of a mile to the closest Shell gas station. He asked the Caucasian female attendant to kindly call his daughter's mother to pick up the child while he figured out what he would do with the car – it was on a Saturday, so no mechanic shop was open. The young lady picked up the phone and was about to make the call – a local call at no cost. This was before cell phones were in the area.

As the young lady was dialing the number, a Caucasian man walked in, presumably the manager or owner. He roughly asked the young lady what she was doing. Evidently, he thought she was assisting the man with the broken-down car because he was standing on the customer's side of the counter eagerly waiting to take the phone from her as soon as his daughter's mother answered the phone. The evidently frightened young lady told the boss that she was making a call for the man with the child now at his side. "Don't do it. Put the phone down. Let him go and find a phone somewhere else," was the angry response of the boss.

This man was not from Mississippi and had not experienced such cruelty before, especially as it relates to a little innocent child. He, while sharing the incident, stressed that he could hardly constrain himself and the evil thoughts that entered his mind. Not so much because his ego was hurt, but because he had his little daughter who would be suffering in the heat as he carried her to some other place to find a telephone. He eventually found a place where he made the call.

The anger caused by the incident raged in the young man for quite a while. Every time he passed the Shell gas station, he would vividly re-live the incident. If you are a father or a mother, you will empathize with the righteous indignation of that young man. A good parent will do whatever is necessary to protect his or her child, especially a young and innocent child.

Only after prayers, meditation, and studying teachings on forgiveness in the Bible was he able to forgive the ungodly man and to pray for him. Such forgiveness was only possible through the Spirit of God in the young man and his desire to forgive.

The young man gives praise and thanks to God for preventing him from responding in a violent manner when he and, more so, his five-year-old daughter were treated so harshly by the owner or manager of the Shell gas station. More importantly, he thanked God for enabling him to forgive the man and to pray for him. May the story of this young man inspire your heart to have the desire to forgive, and may you seek God's assistance when you need to forgive.

Struggling With Forgiving Someone!

You may be struggling with 'good' reasons for not wanting to forgive someone for an 'unforgivable atrocity toward you. You feel justified in your attitude and behavior. But since forgiveness is the ticket that takes you to the Door which leads to the Door to the Kingdom of God, you must forgive. Your situations and circumstances might be quite different from mine and may even be worse and more egregious than mine. Nevertheless, you must forgive if you want God to forgive you. I share my experiences with you, so you will remember that your situations are not unique to you in their hurtfulness. The great news is that you don't have to forgive your own volition alone.

The Teacher Who Forgives Her Malicious Supervisor-School Superintendent

This is the story of the teacher in her own words. She said to herself, "You can't steal my Joy because I won't let you." Neither would she allow the school superintendent to intimidate her nor prevent her from doing the best she could for her students, who she affectionately referred to as her children. When she shared her story with me, I asked her if she would write it so I could include it in this book on forgiveness. Her story is below in her own unedited words.

"The journey wasn't easy… Forgiveness set me free!"

Jan (not her real name) worked in a school district with an enrollment of 2,000 students located in South Mississippi. She taught in this district for twelve (12) years. She had a passion for teaching and dedicated much time to her profession while in the classroom and brought work home to ensure that her students would become lifelong learners. The students loved her. She was well-respected by her peers. The administrator often boasted of what a great job she was doing and often referred to her as a 'Master Teacher.' However, Jan used the phrase every day as she arrived to work and got out of the car – "Lord, don't let nothing happen today that WE can't handle."

The Calm Before The Storm

Everything was going great. Jan was appointed to several committees. She often served as a presenter during professional development workshops-- to model teaching strategies she used in her classroom. Her first teaching assignment was First Grade. Jan taught 1st grade for 3 years. The principal would sing her praises and appoint her grade chair. Everything was going fine as long as Jan danced to the music of the principal and didn't disagree with her.

The Storm Begins

Strike #1: Reporting A Situation A Child-Student Had Experienced

Jan made her first mistake in her 3rd year of teaching 1st grade when she reported to the principal when that it seemed to be a problem with one of her students. The child told her that he couldn't write today because his hand was hurting. Being empathetic and motherly, Jan went to the student's desk to speak with him. She immediately noticed marks that appeared to be bruises on his hand and arms. Jan prepared a report as required by state law and proceeded to the office. Evidently, the principal did not agree with Jan's report and started to dispute with Jan.

The Animosity Toward Jan Begins

Now the animosity starts. Jan was no longer the "Super Teacher" she had always been. She was now the 'smart cookie' in a sarcastic way. Jan was moved to another grade and was assigned the academically lower-performing students. Jan accepted the assignment as a challenge. The students showed much academic growth during the school year.

Strike #2: Jan Is Too Collegial With The Principal

The next school term, the principal, was appointed superintendent. The school got a new principal. She was young, eager to work, energetic, and brought innovative ideas with her. Jan was excited about the new school year, the new principal, and new ideas. She started mixed groups, writing and learning centers, peer tutoring/teaching, critical thinking modules, and hands-on-learning.

Jan became a member of the school's Leadership Team and worked closely with the principal as the lead teacher of the grade she was assigned by the former principal – now superintendent. The superintendent started annoying the principal because she – the superintendent-- wanted things to remain as they were when she was the principal. She told the principal, "If it's fixed, don't break it, or if it's not broken, don't try to fix it."

It appeared that the superintendent had a problem with the relationship Jan had with the principal. The superintendent requested that Jan come to her office for a meeting during Jan's planning period. To Jan's dismay, the meeting was about the principal. The superintendent told Jan that she couldn't be loyal to her and be the principal's friend, too. Jan was shocked by the immature statement. She smiled. The superintendent told her she was waiting on a response. Jan remarked that she reports working on time and most of the time before time; she stays in her room, provides quality instruction to her students, and works late if needed. She gives her job 100% while at work, and when it's time to leave the campus – her job is done. She told the superintendent that she couldn't choose her friends or associates. Just because she had a problem with the principal, she didn't have to have one. The superintendent instructed the new principal to assign Jan to a different grade level – moving her from 2nd grade to 5th and from her area of expertise which was language arts, to math and social science.

Strike 3: Preparing Too Well For Parents And Students

New school year and a new principal. Jan knew the new principal and had previously assisted him with collegiate projects and worked along with him as a teacher. However, he was instructed to move Jan to another grade level and to have her teach in two areas of subjects she had never taught before. The principal notified Jan of the new assignment during the summer.

Jan started preparing her new classroom after July 4th – getting ready for the new school year. She spent her money and countless hours cleaning, painting, decorating the room, and collecting donations (desks, file cabinets, shelves, school supplies, etc.). It was all decked out, and she was ready to meet her new students.

The new school year started. The school scheduled 'Parent-Teacher Orientation' and 'Meet Your Child's Teacher' for the day before the students were to arrive. Jan received her students' roster prior to the first day of school. She had labeled each desk with the student's name and placed a 'Welcome' folder for the parents on their child's assigned seat. The folder contained contact information and skills to be taught during the year. She also had a bag with goodies for each parent. In addition, Jan was preparing refreshments for her parents. Jan was ready to greet parents and eager to teach her students.

Then Jan had a surprise visit the day before 'Meet You Child's Teacher' day. The superintendent and her assistant walked into the classroom. They were mesmerized by Jan's classroom. They took a seat in one of the learning centers and invited Jan to come and join them. Jan complied.

The superintendent told Jan that she was going to say something that she didn't want to hear, but she had no choice. Jan looked stunned, wondering what else could happen. Then the blow came--you had to move to another school--they need you over there. Jan was flabbergasted. This was the first time they saw her sweat. She placed her head on the table, cupped it with her hands, and cried like a baby.

Jane couldn't believe they would do her that way--after spending time and money getting the classroom ready. And it was the day before school would begin. If that wasn't bad enough, she reported to the other school the next day to a room with a broken air conditioner.

To add injury to insult, without Jan's knowledge, the superintendent registered for 6-week in-service training, which was scheduled on Saturdays. The in-service training would enable Jan to become certified and receive an endorsement in the subject areas to which she was assigned.

Jan Used Bitter Lemons To Make Lemonade

Jan held classes in the auditorium for 1 ½ month before returning to the classroom. She said she took lemons and made lemonade. She successfully completed the stressful school year.

God Had A Plan For Jan

God had something better for Jan. She obtained a new job teaching 1st grade, and that was only five minutes away from home. Later she was promoted to become an administrator at the school

Jan Forgives The Superintendent And Is Joyful

Two years after Jan left the school, where the superintendent treated her unfairly, she came face to face with the superintendent. Jan greeted her as if nothing despiteful had ever happened. They exchanged small talk and ended their conversation with Jan forgiving and embracing the superintendent. Jan said that she had a joyful feeling. Forgiveness was demonstrated by action.

Jan remarked that after all she had been through, nothing was going to steal her joy. She was instructed by the teaching of the Apostle Paul, **"And be ye kind one to another, tenderhearted, forgiving one another, even as God for Christ's sake hath forgiven you"** (Ephesians 4:32, KJV)

I have included your experiences with Jan in this book, hoping that they might be a blessing and encouragement to you. Perhaps you will be inspired to reflect on your life and write your own story of how you have forgiven someone. May God help you in so doing!

Cruelty And Forgiveness That Will Make You Cry And Pray!

I affectionately call her the Dancing Song Bird. When she shared a life experience with me, I was truly moved to tears. I asked her if she would like to include it in my book of forgiveness so that it might be a blessing to others. She agreed. Her story, in her own words, follows.

Forgiven And Almost Forgotten

What is forgiveness? What does it mean to you? I believe forgiveness is the act of releasing all negative emotions towards something or someone that has wronged us. One of the most profound memories of forgiveness I recall is the story of my friend Pinky. She described the experience as one of the worst times of her life. She was about 20 years old and pregnant with her first child. Four years earlier

Pinky's mother had been diagnosed with Alzheimer's. Pinky's new journey and the experience was one usually chartered by 'mother.' A new and expecting mother usually looks to her mom for guidance, comfort, and support during this time. That opportunity was snatched from Pinky way too early. I could see it in her eyes--that longing for a mother-daughter relationship.

Pinky was young, and she didn't know what to do or how to deal with pregnancy, so she sought that support from the closest thing to her mother that she could find. Jane, her sister, was the eldest of three girls alive. They had buried their eldest brother (her mother's first child) about three months earlier. He was shot and killed by gunmen for undetermined motives.

Jane is concerned about her sister Pinky inviting her to stay at her house until she has her baby. Jane has a rough character – some would even say that she was mean-spirited. One had to be careful when dealing with her. Pinky was unemployed and didn't have the support of the baby's father, so she had to rely on her sister Jane for almost everything. I can imagine that it wasn't easy for Jane to support Pinky financially totally, especially because she didn't have the perfect job and she wasn't rich.

In the 7th month of her pregnancy, Pinky experienced something almost tragic. One evening Jane came home from work and saw that Pinky had prepared a meal. Jane, without gratitude or empathy, considered the meal disgusting since it was not done to her liking; she burst into a negative argument.

Jane was very upset about the macaroni and cheese and what she considered the excess moisture in the food. She expressed her dissatisfaction and anger in a very blunt and aggressive manner. Pinky being under her pregnant hormones, reacted with anger which fueled the conflict. Jane, who never backs down from a challenge, blazed with anger and threw a slap in Pinky's face.

Jane and her pregnant sister Pinky started tussling. In the midst of the fuss, Jane said to Pinky," Do you think because you are pregnant, I am afraid to slap you in your 'rass.' Jane then punched Pinky in her belly. At that moment, Pinky began feeling cramps and was wetting herself. And then Pinky walked away from the fight. The cramps kept coming and were getting stronger, and at that point, Pinky thought she was about to lose her baby, so she called the father of the child to come and get her.

Pinky spent almost a month in the hospital while the nurses tried to prevent the baby from being born prematurely at six months and possibly dying. Pinky fought through the difficult time, and both she and that baby lived. Pinky pledged to herself and her baby at the baby's birth that she would never talk to her sister, never, ever again, because of what she did to her.

The Life-Changing Decision To Forgive

Although Pinky had pledged to never talk with her eldest sister again, about a year after the baby was born, Pinky made a life-changing decision to let go of the hurt and forgive her sister. Pinky had grown to recognize that forgiveness is necessary for the forgiver much more than it is for the one being forgiven. How is that even possible? One would ask. Well, when we choose to forgive, we take control of our own lives as unforgiveness robs us of our God-given power to steer our lives in a positive direction. Forgiveness gives you a healthy heart literally! The less we hold on to baggage, dramas, and trauma, the more we can relax and enjoy life.

By now, I know my readers are wondering how it is that I knew so much about Pinky. Well, that's because Pinky is my best friend; Pinky is me! I found that after being able to let go of the blade of a sharpened knife, I didn't feel the pain anymore. I don't have my mother to speak to for guidance towards any important aspect of my life, but I have an elder sister that I can reach out to, somebody I can turn to just to speak and clear my mind when it feels like I just don't know what else.

I have Abounding peace from such an experience, and that is enough for me. As for my sister, she is still far away from perfect or a peaceful character; however, I have managed to share with her on different occasions why we have to sometimes bite our lips and make a deliberate effort to propel peace and oneness amongst ourselves as the Bible says a soft answer turneth away wrath, but grievous words stir up anger. I am still learning and growing in this whole process; however, I know how cruel this world can be when you don't have strong family support, and so I am grateful for the relationship we currently share. Forgiveness heals your heart and opens up a whole world of abundance to a fulfilling life.

PS: She leaves my dinner every single time I say I am coming home, even though she knows I have a tendency to not show up because I lead a busy life. 😊

Chapter 12

Father, Please Help Me Forgive Him

The Miracle of Forgiveness

As previously mentioned, God placed Adam in the Garden of Eden as the Steward. God told Adam, **"Of every tree thou mayest eat: But of the tree of the knowledge of the good and evil, thou shall not eat of it: for the day that thou eatest thereof though shalt surely die" Genesis 2:16 – 17).** God gave that instruction to Adam before He created Eve to be Adam's helpmate. The instruction was clear, and God was kind enough to inform Adam of the existential consequence of disobeying the instruction – yet Adam chose to disobey God. Adam earned the consequence of his disobedience. However, the God of love – God who is Love extended grace and mercy to Adam but did not remove all consequences from Adam.

God extended the miracle of forgiveness, with a severe consequence, to Adam. He spared Adam from immediate physical death but did not spare him from immediate spiritual death. And God forgives Adam and symbolizes His forgiveness by shedding the blood of an innocent animal to make a coat to protect Adam and one for Eve, his wife as well. The slaying of the innocent animal was a precursor of the innocent Son of God giving up His life to forgive and save humanity. That is the miracle of forgiveness.

It was a miracle that God spared and forgave Adam, and it is a miracle that God spares and forgives you and me. Because we, too, have sinned and disobeyed God, and the wages of sin is death. Therefore, we have earned the consequence of sin – spiritual death. Nevertheless, through the miracle of the death and resurrection of Jesus, God spares and forgives our sins. It is truly a miracle how God changed a consequence of sin – death to eternal life through the death and resurrection of Jesus.

So despite your hurt and suffering, you must ask God to please help you to extend to others the type of forgiveness that God extends to you. I have said it previously; however, it's worth repeating. The forgiveness which you want to extend might require a miracle – God's intervention. So you earnestly ask God to instill in your heart the desire and willingness to forgive in the specific seemingly 'unforgivable' situation or person(s). And you expect that God will assist you. Then you act with confidence that God has answered your prayer. You then thank God for answering your prayer. If it is possible, let the offender(s) know that you have forgiven him, her, or them.

You will feel the weight and bitterness falling from you as Saul felt the scales falling from his eyes when Ananias said to him, "Brother Saul, receive your sight." In truth and in fact, you will receive a heightened vision of the love, mercy, grace, and forgiveness of God.

I write this short chapter on the importance of asking God to help you forgive to reemphasize that you really need a miracle to be able to forgive some atrocities, pains, and hurt that you endure. The God who raises you from spiritual death to eternal life is able to help you forgive in a particular situation as well as create a forgiving heart in you. Accept the miracle of forgiveness and forgive.

Chapter 13

The Joy Of Forgiving

Rejoice in the Lord

I wrote this introductory paragraph to this chapter after I had selected the title of the chapter and was well into writing the subheadings, but then something interesting happened. I was doing my early morning daily devotion on July 23, 2021, using the 2021 Annual Edition of "Our Daily Bread." To my amazement and an affirmation to me, the Bible reading came from Psalm 33:6 – 13 – and the title of Psalm 33 in the King James Version (KJV) is "The Joy of Forgiveness" – the title I had already chosen for this chapter, as noted above. I had to read Psalm 33 several times in order to grip the joy of forgiveness to which the writer of Psalm 33, KJV, refers. I have incorporated thoughts from Psalm 33 in this chapter of the book, which certainly enriches this chapter and enthralls your joy of forgiving.

Psalm 33 reminds us, **"REJOICE in the Lord. O ye righteous (believer): for praise is comely for the upright (believer). For our heart shall rejoice in him, because we have trusted in his holy name. Let thy mercy, O LORD, be up on us, according as we hope in thee" (Psalm 33:1, 22 – 22).** The Psalmist encourages, in fact, urges believers in God to sing joyfully to God because it is appropriate and mandatory to praise God (Psalm 150:6).. The Psalmist goes on to say that you and I should rejoice – have joy in God because we trust in Him. In addition, the Psalmist prays that the mercy of God is upon those in hope in God. It is that trust and hope in God which allows the believer-you, me to have unwavering confidence that God enables you to forgive, even the seemingly 'unforgivable' – the most depraved. With forgiveness comes great joy!

No Longer Shackled By Guilt

In the previous chapter, I urged you to ask God to help you forgive and to give you a forgiving heart. Because you believe, you can rest assured that God has answered your prayer. And you are walking in faith to 'make an effort' to forgive even the seemingly 'unforgivable.' And to your pleasant surprise, you realized that you were able to forgive because it is the Spirit of God who is in you who gives you the ability to forgive (Philippians 2:13; 4:13).

How do you feel? Or how did you feel the moment you forgave? Undoubtedly, a burden has been lifted from you – you feel lighter and guiltless – as a Christian-believer, you felt some guilt because you have been crying out – and probably 'rightly so' – for revenge and justice, and somehow you knew that was not right. It is said that forgiveness is the most effective antidote against the venom of hate and bitterness and the desire for vengeance and demand for revenge. You have turned over any vengeance or revenge to God – that is His business – He says, "Vengeance is mine, He will deal with it" (Deuteronomy 32:35; Romans 12:7). Yet the merciful God is "Slow to anger and quick to forgive (Psalm 103:8; 145:8; 1 John 1:9).

Now, the desires for revenge and even for justice are replaced with a desire for mercy and a feeling of love for the offender(s). You have overcome your annoying bitterness, and you are no longer trapped in a feeling of being violated. You have taken the higher ground; because God has answered your prayer. And you feel a sense of calm and peace of mind. You are no longer shackled to your anger, bitterness, your sense of being violated, and being shackled-chained by your offender(s). Your desire for revenge has been transformed formed to a prayer of forgiveness. Your conscience is clear; your guilt is gone, and you did not transfer your guilt to your offender(s), who you once thought needed to carry that burden. Rather, you left your guilt at the place where God answered your prayer – in God's hands.

Free At Last, Thank God, I Am Free

When the British Parliament passed the law to abolish slavery in all British colonies in 1838, the slavery abolitionist William Wilberforce is quoted as saying, "Free at last, free at last, thank God Almighty we are free at last. "

Well, with the relinquishing of your feelings of anguish, anger, disdain, resentment, and so forth – which were precipitated by the atrocities of your terrible offender(s) – and replacing those feelings with forgiveness, you more than likely feel free. Perhaps you feel as free as William Wilberforce felt when he learned that the British Parliament had passed the Abolition of Slavery Act. In fact, your freedom is physical and emotional, but especially spiritual – so you are truly free indeed.

Yes, forgiving someone does give you that feeling of being free – a free conscience, free from guilt and from emotional and spiritual burdens. So you can say with a feeling of heightened satisfaction cushioned with humility, "Thank God Almighty, I am free from the shackle of unforgiveness, and I am enjoying the freedom which forgiveness has ushered into my heart, mind, and spirit.

Full Of Joy

In one of my previous books, "Becoming a Joy-Fulfilled Christian in the Twenty-First Century and Beyond...." I urged followers of Jesus to appropriate and fully utilize the joy which Jesus makes available to them. As a follower of Jesus, when you forgive others, and God forgives you, the joy of Jesus can be fulfilled in you. Jesus links His joy to love. He said, **"These things I have spoken unto you, that my joy might remain in you, and that your joy might be full. This is my commandment, That ye love one another, as I have loved you"** (Luke 15:11 – 12). I previously stated that love precedes true forgiveness. God extended His love to humanity and gave His Son as a sacrifice for our sins so that He is able to forgive you and me (John 3:16).

It is quite clear that Jesus wants His followers to be full of joy. As stated previously, asking God to help you forgive others and to give you a forgiving heart is essential for your joy-fulfilled earthly life and for your eternal life.

Jesus admonishes His disciples-followers, **"Hitherto have ye asked nothing in my name: ask, and ye shall receive, that your joy may be full"** Luke 16:24). Jesus repeats His desire that you have His full joy in you – joy which is now available to you while you are on earth as His follower. However, you have the free will to accept or reject the deep-down joy that Jesus alone provides. This joy comes when you accept Jesus as your Savior and obey His instructions and expect the joy with confidence.

Within a short period of time, after Jesus admonishes His disciples to ask and have His joy fulfilled in them, He prays to His Father on behalf of His disciples, **"And come I to thee; and these things I speak in the world, that they might have my joy fulfilled in themselves' (John 17:13).** In this prayer, Jesus indicates that He was not only praying for the existing disciples, but for all those who will believe in Him because of the words of the disciples who existed then. Therefore, Jesus prayed for you and me. Jesus prays, **"Neither pray I for these (disciples) alone, but for them also which shall believe on me through their word" (John 17:20).**

Because you believe in God, trust God, and pray to God in the name of Jesus, Jesus' joy is available to you, but you must claim it. Jesus has already prayed that His joy will be in you. However, you must believe in Jesus, and you must forgive those who hurt you. I want to repeat and emphasize that **it is the Spirit of Jesus that is in you** that provides you with both the desire and ability – **the miracle to forgive** the seemingly 'impossible' – to forgive the 'unforgivable.' What a mighty God and a loving and forgiving Savior!

Double Blessings: To the Forgiver and the Forgiven

Forgiveness brings about a double blessing, analogous to the blessing Portia mentioned in Shakespeare's Merchant of Venice: "It (mercy) is twice blessed. It blesseth him that gives and him that takes. " Similarly, forgiveness is a blessing to the person who forgives and the one who is forgiven. I have mentioned some of the benefits of forgiveness to the forgiver previously. However, consider the composite spiritual blessing you receive when God forgives you – eternal life. There is no gift that can be compared with the gift of eternal. And the thesis of this book is that **Forgiveness is the key that opens the Door-Jesus to eternal life.**

Chapter 14

Conclusion

The Consequences of Unforgiveness

This is the most important and consequential book I have written so far. As stated in the introduction, I am extremely spiritually burdened by persons, 'Christians' – 'good' persons – who struggle with the idea that they must forgive others if they want God to forgive them. I am even more worried about those who say, "I will forgive him or her, but I will never forget what he or she did to me." What this means is that when the forgiver of the 'difficult-to-forgive' comes in contact with or hears the name of the 'difficult-to-forgive' ('unforgivable'), the forgiver's heart races, and he or she recalls the terrible atrocities which the 'unforgivable' offender inflicted on the would-be forgiver – directly or indirectly. Often, the forgiver (victim) has not really and truly forgiven the offender at all.

I have purposefully repeated some concepts and or admonitions, on forgiveness, in this section of the book for emphasis. Because I want you to appreciate the fact that forgiveness is crucial to salvation. **However, forgiveness does not necessarily eliminate accountability nor totally exonerate one from the consequences of unacceptable behavior.** God frequently mitigates consequences but often holds people accountable, even when He fully forgives them. The repetitions are for your benefit.

So, as a Christian-believer, if you are not prepared to imitate God by forgiving the offender and forgetting the offenses perpetrated against you, you are risking not using the key which opens the Door (Jesus Christ), allowing you to enter the Kingdom of God. Jesus said, **"I am the door: by me if any man enter in, he shall be saved, and shall go in and out, and find pasture" (John 10:9).** I am not simply saying that you are at risk of not entering the Kingdom of God if you refuse to forgive others, just because I want to scare you. Jesus, Himself says, **"If ye forgive not men their trespasses, neither will your heavenly Father forgive your trespasses" (Matthew 6:15).** Without God's forgiveness, you and I can in no way enter the Kingdom of God, regardless of our 'righteousness' – good deeds. Because you and I have sinned and fallen short of God's holiness (Romans 3:23). And the wages of sin is death – loss of eternal life Romans 6:23).

The unforgiving attitude of many Christian-believers – even those with seemingly 'good' intentions – burdens my heart. The 'good' intention of "I will forgive and forget someday" is not enough. Or, perhaps worse, "I will forgive, but I will never forget." Your 'good' intention must be transmuted into action by your free will, your desire, and the Spirit of Jesus in you. One of my mentors, who became my employee, frequently commented that "The road to hell (hades) is paved with good intention." When you have the Spirit of Jesus in you, if you desire to forgive by your free will, the Spirit of Jesus will aid you in forgiving.

Every time I hear a Christian believer proclaims that I will forgive him or her or them, but I will never, never forget," I am reminded of a preacher in Franklin County. The preacher preached a sermon entitled "The Man Whom God Forgot." The essence of the sermon was that when God forgives a man (person) of his or her sins, God does not remember that sinful man (person) any more. The forgiven person is 'new,' justified by God as being righteous in God's sight. So, God forgives the sinful acts of the forgiven person and replaces that person with the 'new' born-again person. The preacher does have a point – God forgives and forgets because He is God.

You might rightly argue that God is holy and can do all that He chooses to do, and you are just a mere born-again Christian-believer. You are correct; however, as a believer in Jesus-His follower, Jesus has expectations of you – which the Holy Spirit assists you in accomplishing. Moses puts one super-important expectation of God this way, **"Ye shall be holy: for I the LORD is holy" (Leviticus 19:2).** Centuries after Moses' admonition to the children of Israel, the Apostle Peter proclaimed to Christians-followers of Jesus, **"But as he which hath called you is holy, so be ye holy in all manner of conversation (living" (1 Peter 1:15).** Jesus does not ask His followers to do anything which He-the Holy Spirit will not assist them to do – including humanly impossible things, such as being holy as His Father – if the followers ask and trust and expect with confidence. This includes the miracle of true and total forgiveness.

Of course, a born-again person – a Christian-believer – the new creation – wants to forgive the offender and prayerfully forget the offenses. I take great comfort in knowing that God will help those who want to forgive the offender and forget the offenses do so. However, a Christian-believer has an obligation to study, pray, meditate, and even fast in order to grow spiritually; so that forgiving others will not be so difficult – especially to forgive seventy times seven – as often as the offender commits offenses and seeks forgiveness. It is the Spirit of Jesus in the believer which makes such forgiveness possible.

As I previously stated, Jesus gives the admonition to believers to forgive others; however, He did not revoke the free will to forgive or not forgive. It is difficult or perhaps even impossible for a non-believer or not-yet-believer to forgive to the extent that believers are able to forgive. Again, it is the Spirit of Jesus in the believer which makes true forgiveness possible.

The admonition or exhortation to the not-yet believer is **"That if thou shall confess with thy mouth the Lord Jesus Christ, and shall believe in thine heart that God hath raised him, from the dead, thou shalt be saved" (Romans 10:9).** It is very important to remember that it is the believer whom Jesus asks to forgive others. They need God's forgiveness continuously, and they, with the Spirit of Jesus in them, are able to forgive totally and completely. The first task of the not-yet believer is to accept Jesus as Savior. See above.

Clearly, there are not-yet believers who forgive others as they choose. However, forgiving others is not optional for believers who are seeking to enter the Kingdom of God. Rather, it is a quintessential requirement. Believers live in a sinful world and face demonic challenges regularly; therefore, they are subject to temptation and often yield. Consequently, believers must constantly seek God's forgiveness. But as I have previously mentioned, forgiving others is a prerequisite for believers who are seeking God's forgiveness. Jesus expresses the prerequisite for God's forgiveness in this manner, **"For if ye forgive men their trespasses, your heavenly Father will also forgive you: But if ye forgive**

not men their trespasses, neither will your Father forgive your trespasses" (Matthew 6:14 – 15).

How is it possible to comply with the teaching of Jesus that you forgive someone who has willfully and deliberately committed some egregious atrocity against you or against someone you dearly love – such as your mother or your beloved child? Well, the truth of the matter is that the admonition to forgive might seem impossible to the natural person, who may try to comply of his or her own volition. And it might indeed be impossible for such a person, even a 'good' person, to manifest by his or her volition the type of forgiveness Jesus demands. However, there is a way. A miracle might be required – Jesus 'intervention.

For the believer, it is the Spirit of Jesus in him or her which turns human's impossibility into God's possibility. As Jesus reminds His disciples, **"With men this is impossible; but with God all things are possible" (Matthew 19:26; Mark10:27)**.

I have previously said that Jesus' instruction to forgive is probably one of Jesus's most difficult instructions to execute. The Apostle Paul mentions that he was able to do things by the grace of God – perhaps he even prayed to those who had stoned him at Lystra during his First Missionary Journey and left him for dead (Acts 14:19). He gives credit to the Spirit which enabled him to do great things (spiritual and temporal) in this way, **"Yet not I, but the grace of God which was in me" (1 Corinthians 15:10).**

Remember my emphasis in this book that forgiveness is the key that opens the Door-Jesus to eternal life. Without God's forgiveness, one cannot get through the Door-Jesus into God's Kingdom-Eternal Life. No wonder throughout this book, I have stressed the importance of believers forgiving one another and forgiving others – even not-yet believers.

The hallmark of a born-again Christian-believer is the willingness to forgive, not only in words and deeds; rather, more importantly, in the heart. And to experience Jesus' joy-feeling good about forgiving others. I have previously said that forgiving others is one of the most difficult and consequential assignments that Jesus has given each of His followers, regardless of the follower-believer or the person who needs forgiveness – a believer or a not-yet believer. This assignment to forgive will only be successfully completed when the Spirit of Jesus-God is in the follower-believer, and the follower-believer exercises his or her free will to forgive. Then the Spirit will do the rest.

The successful completion of this life-or-death assignment requires the unwavering cooperation of the believer with the Holy Spirit – the Spirit of Jesus-God – who is already inside the born-again believer.

It is important to remind the reader that the not-yet believer needs only to accept Jesus Christ as his or her Lord and Savior in order to be saved – to become a believer and to receive the Holy (Ghost) Spirit. On the Day of Pentecost, many who heard the preaching of Peter's first sermon were pricked in their heart (convicted) and asked, **"Men and brethren, what shall we do? Then Peter said unto them, Repent and be baptized every one of you in the name of Jesus Christ for the remission of your sins, and ye shall receive the gift of the Holy Ghost"** (Act 2:37 – 28).

It is conceivable that not-yet believers can accept Jesus Christ as Lord and Savior even though they have not yet forgiven someone who has trespassed against them. The Apostle Paul teaches that the process of accepting Jesus Christ as Lord and Savior (and receiving the Holy Spirit) is quite straightforward. He puts it this way, **"That if thou shalt confess with thy mouth the Lord Jesus, and shall believe in thine heart that God hath raised him from the dead, thou shalt be saved" (Romans 10:9).** Once the formerly not-yet believer has accepted Jesus Christ as Lord and Savior, that person is transformed into a believer-a Christian. Then and only then can that new person – the born-again believer – truly forgives others for their trespasses in the manner Jesus requires.

There are two quintessential points I reiterate here that you – the reader – must remember. Firstly, you should not expect the not-yet believer to do the impossible for the not-yet believer – to forgive others in the manner Jesus expects – seventy times seven for every infraction – as often as the perpetrator seeks forgiveness.

Secondly, as soon as one accepts Jesus Christ as Lord and Savior, the Holy Spirit enters that born-again believer and empowers the believer with the ability to forgive in the manner that Jesus requires of believers-His followers. The bottom line is that, on the one hand, not-yet believers do not yet possess the indwelling of the Holy Spirit and do not possess the ability to forgive in the manner Jesus requires. On the other hand, true believers possess the Holy Spirit; hence, they have the capacity to forgive as Jesus requires. However, believers still have free will and can choose to forgive or not to forgive, despite the urging of the Holy Spirit to forgive.

You cannot read and should not try to read the heart of a believer or the heart of anyone, for that matter. However, you can hear his or he words, observe the behaviors, and in many cases, detect the attitude. Therefore, you might have a good feeling as to whether a believer has a forgiving disposition. In addition, the Holy Spirit in you will assist you in discerning much about others. Jesus instructs the believers-His followers: **"Let your light so shine before men, that they may see your good works and glorify your Father which is in heaven" (Matthew 5:16).** So, believers in Jesus will demonstrate that the Spirit of Jesus is in them by their good deeds, their kind words, and their positive attitude and respect for others. The Holy Spirit will assist other believers in discerning the Holy Spirit in you and vice versa. They and you will have an attitude of true forgiveness.

Those who possess the Spirit of God-Jesus possess the capacity to forgive others for their trespasses; however, you and I must nurture and cultivate the desire to forgive. And the best way to forgive is to pray about the situation, forgive, then turn the matter over to God. We believe that when we genuinely repent and forgive others and seek God's forgiveness, God forgives our trespasses and remembers those trespasses no more. He does not bring up forgiven trespasses every time we commit new trespass against Him.

Believers are **"Saved by grace through faith and not by works, lest any man should boast" (Ephesians 2:8 – 9).** However, despite our best efforts, we continually fall short of God's expectations of us. As stated previously, the Apostle Paul reminds us, **"For all have sinned, and come short of the glory of God" (Romans 3:23).** And those who desire eternal life must seek God's forgiveness over and over and over again. Because we sin over and over again. The Apostle John reminds us, **"If**

we confess our sins, he is faithful and just to forgive us our sins, and to cleanse us from all unrighteousness" (1 John 1:9). God continues to extend His grace to us. In fact, Paul teaches that God extends abundant grace to us to cover our sins, **"But where sin abounded, (God's) grace did much more abound. That as sin hath reigned unto death, even so might grace reign through righteousness unto eternal by Jesus Christ our Lord" (Romans 5:20 – 21).** God provides abundant grace through the sacrificial death of His Son to make salvation-forgiveness available to all who choose to exercise a little faith in Jesus – as much as a grain of mustard and to seek God's forgiveness.

Nevertheless, God, Jesus, or the Holy Spirit will not force you or anyone else to accept Jesus as your Lord or Savior or to forgive others for their trespasses. It is all up to you and me to accept Jesus, develop an attitude of forgiveness, and minister to others. If we believe in Jesus and the importance of forgiveness, we have a moral responsibility, and perhaps a spiritual responsibility as well, to share our beliefs regarding forgiveness with other believers and not-yet believers. You and I must especially practice and model the essence of true forgiveness as demonstrated by Jesus, Stephen, and Paul in their lives and death.

As a Christian-believer, you must make an intentional decision to forgive and do your part to reach and assist those in your orbit which will 'lend you their ears!'

Forgiveness with Consequences: Old Testament Examples

Some people, especially those who are not yet believers, have a difficult time understanding how an 'evil person could get forgiveness for some heinous atrocity without any consequence at all. I want to reemphasize that forgiveness does not necessarily exonerate – provide proof of innocence; hence eliminate all consequences relative to the offense. As I write this chapter of this book on forgiveness, there are many debates and questioning going on in the United States of America and in other countries regarding alleged crimes and infractions that seem to go unpunished. There are cries everywhere for justice and accountability.

I will use a few examples from the Bible to illustrate that, on numerous occasions, individuals received forgiveness but were held accountable. In many cases, consequences were mitigated by God's grace and mercy. There were times when God Himself granted forgiveness (implicit or explicit) and concomitantly executed consequences with grace and mercy. I provide the following examples, some of which were discussed in a previous chapter of the book.

Adam and Eve

Adam disobeyed God's instruction not to eat the fruit of a certain tree in the Garden of Eden. Adam, in effect, rebelled against God – he sinned. The normal result of such disobedience-sin was immediate spiritual and physical death. This was an egregious infraction against God, considering Adam and his wife. Eve obeyed the devil over God.

God was angry with Adam and could have executed spiritual and physical death; however, God was merciful to them and spared their physical life. God forgives the disobedience, rebellion, and sin of Adam as far as immediate physical death is concerned. In fact, God showed great mercy toward Adam and Eve by sacrificing or killing an animal and using the skin to make coats for them. But God did not exonerate them completely from the consequence of their disobedience. He sent them away from the beautiful Garden of Eden. So, Adam had to till the soil to grow crops for food, and Eve was subjugated to Adam and would endure pains when she gave birth to children. (Genesis Chapter 3).

Yes, the merciful God held Adam and Eve accountable for their rebellion, even though they did not receive the full consequences for their rebellion against God. So the idea of some that forgiveness nullifies accountability is neither scriptural nor moral. There must be forgiveness, especially when there is acceptance of responsibility, sincere and remorseful repentance, and an appeal for forgiveness. But even so, forgiveness does not mean the elimination of accountability and (all) applicable consequences.

Rebekah and Jacob (Israel)

You will more than likely recall how Rebekah conspired with her favorite son Jacob to deceive her husband Isaac, Jacob's father, to steal away Esau's (special) blessing. Jacob was somewhat hesitant to go along with the scheme. He was afraid to go along with his mother's plot for fear that his father would detect the fraud and pronounce a curse on him instead of a blessing. However, Rebekah convinced him to cooperate with the plot, indicating that if there was a curse, she would take it all.

The plot worked even though Isaac was skeptical that the imposter – Jacob he was about to bless was not Esau, his elder, and favorite son. Well, Jacob lied to his father with the assistance of Rebekah, his mother. He received Esau's blessing but had to run away from home because he was afraid that Esau might kill him.

God forgave Jacob and, more than likely forgave Rebekah as well. However, they suffered consequences for their deception. Jacob was away from his father for twenty years and away from his mother as long as she was alive. In addition, there is no indication in the Bible that Jacob and Rebekah ever saw each other again. Rebekah died without laying eyes on the son she loved so much. (Genesis Chapters 27 – 29; 33) That was a severe consequence for Rebekah and her beloved son Jacob.

Years later, Jacob suffered a consequential and heartrending experience-deception. As Jacob had conspired with his mother Rebekah to deceive his father Isaac, his sons conspired to deceive him in a most devastating manner. Evidently, Jacob had not learned the danger of showing partiality and preference among children. Among his twelve sons, he showed great partiality and preference for his 11th son Joseph. Joseph's brothers envied (and probably hated him).

Jacob sent Joseph to take food for his brothers, who were taking care of their father's (Jacob's) flock in Shechem. The brothers decided to violate Joseph – to sell him and to deceive their father.

The brother, Reuben, was not present at the time the other brothers sold Joseph to Ishmaelites who were heading for Egypt. Then they dipped Joseph's coat of many colors – the symbol of Jacob's preferential love for

Joseph – in the blood of a kid (goat or sheep). They took the coat to Jacob and lied to him that they had found the coat and did not know if it belonged to his son (Joseph). Jacob's reaction to the deception of his sons was far more devastating and disheartening than the reaction of his father, Isaac, to his and his mother's deception.

When Jacob examined the coat, he exclaimed, **"It is my son's coat: an evil beast hath devoured him; Joseph is without doubt rent in pieces. And Jacob rent his clothes, and put sackcloth upon his loins, and mourned for his sons many days" (Genesis 37:33 – 34).** Jacob received additional consequences for deceiving his father and robbing his brother Esau of his blessing. Nevertheless, God named His special people after Jacob, whose name was changed to Israel – a powerful prince and God's special people were named after him – the children of Israel (Genesis 32:28).

Jacob is a perfect example of a person in the Bible who suffered severe consequences for his behavior even though God forgave his misdeeds and granted him enormous blessings – even naming the nation of Israel after him. No one, not even Jacob, was or is immune to accountability and the consequences of wrongs.

Centuries later, the Apostle Paul wrote, **"Be not deceived; God is not mocked: for whatsoever a man soweth, that shall he also reap" (Galatians 6:7)**. Paul reaped what he sowed

Moses and Aaron

I have discussed Moses at great length in the book. Moses led the children of Israel out of slavery in Egypt and then in the wilderness for forty years. He stood up to Pharaoh and to the rebellious children of Israel. Yet the Bible describes Moses as a humble man, thusly, **"Now the man Moses was very meek, above all men which were upon the face of the earth" (Numbers 12:3)**. So why do I include Moses as one who received God's forgiveness with severe consequence? What did he do, and what was the consequence?

There are two occasions in which Moses, the great and humble leader, seemed to have been overwhelmed by the behaviors – sinfulness, ingratitude, and rebelliousness of the children of Israel as he led them in the wilderness. One occasion was when God gave him the Ten Commandments, written on two tablets by God's own hand, and Moses deliberately broke the tablets by throwing them to the ground when he saw the children of Israel worshipping a golden calf. The second occasion was when God instructed Moose to speak to the rock to obtain water for the murmuring children of Israel, and he struck the rock.

To elaborate on the incidents of Moses and Aaron

Breaking of the Tablets With the Ten Commandments

God called Moses to Mount Sanai, where God wrote the Ten Commandments on two tables of stone (tablets) and gave them to Moses to read to the children of Israel. Moses was on Mount Sanai with God for forty days.

When Moses got off Mount Sanai and reached where the children of Israel were camping. He noticed that the children of Israel were worshipping an idol – a golden calf that Aaron had assisted in making. The children of Israel had broken the first of the Ten Commandments God had just given to Moses: **"Thou shall have no other gods before me" (Exodus 20:3).** Moses was infuriated and full of righteous indignation. His anger got the better of him. He threw down the tablets and broke them (Exodus 32:19). Some people contend that Moses, who had spent forty days in the presence of God, should have exercised better control over his anger. Perhaps, God is a lot more compassionate than mere humans. The Bible does not disclose whether or not God was angry with Moses on this occasion.

Centuries later, a wise man – perhaps Solomon – wrote: **"He that is slow to anger is better than the mighty; and he that keepeth his spirit than he that taketh a city" (Proverbs 16:32).** Evidently, Moses had some difficulty in controlling toward the children of Israel.

Striking of the Rock and Sharing Credit Due to God Alone

The children of Israel were suffering from unbearable thirst in the wilderness. They had no water for some time. God told Moses that he should take his rod and gather Aaron and the children of Israel around the rock and speak to the rock, and the rock – God would provide water. Moses, perhaps out of frustration with the ungrateful children of Israel, gathered them around the rock as God instructed. Then said to them, **"Hear now, ye rebels; must we fetch you water out of this rock? And Moses lifted up his hand, and with the rod he smote the rock twice: and water came out abundantly"** (Numbers 20:10 – 11).

God's reaction to Moses' failure to carry out His precise instruction was prompt and monumental. God held both Moses and Aaron accountable for failing to comply with God's message, which had a significant meaning. God wanted the children of Israel to understand that He was supplying the water. God executed a significant consequence on Moses and Aaron. He told them that because they did not believe in God and had failed to sanctify Him – to set God apart in the eyes of the children of Israel, He would prohibit them from leading the children of Israel into the Promised Land. Not only did Moses strike the rock when God told him to speak to it, but he seemed to have acted as though he was equalizing himself with God in providing the water (Numbers 20:12).

God Held Aaron Accountable

Moses and Aaron led the children of Israel to Mount Hor. God spoke unto Moses and Aaron on Mount Hor, saying, **"Aaron shall be gathered unto his people (shall die): for he shall not enter into the land which I have given unto the children of Israel, because rebelled against my word at the water of Meribah" (Numbers 20:23 – 24).** There is every reason to believe that God forgave Aaron for making the idol-golden calf and engaging the children of Israel in worshipping it. God did not even express His anger at the time. Similarly, God undoubtedly forgave Aaron for standing beside Moses – not discouraging him from striking the rock and the words Moses spoke. However, God did not exonerate Aaron from the consequences of the incident where

Moses struck the rock and shared the credit for the water with God and for not glorifying God in the ears of the people.

Aaron's severe consequences. God told Moses to strip Aaron of his priestly garments and put them on Aaron's son. In addition, Aaron died on Mount Hor. God did not permit him to enter the Promised Land. (Numbers 20:24, 29). This is quite a significant accountability since Aaron was a co-leader, with Moses, of the children of Israel from the time Moses appeared before Pharaoh in Egypt. Forgiveness does not necessarily exonerate one from all consequences of infractions. God held Aaron accountable for his behaviors, which perhaps included the building of the golden idol calf and allowing the children of Israel to worship it.

God Held Moses Accountable

As previously stated, Moses was held accountable and received severe consequences for his behavior at the rock at Meribah. However, God granted grace and mercy in addition to forgiveness to Moses – His great and humble leader. God permitted Moses to see the Promised Land. **"And Moses went up from the plains of Moab unto the mountains of Nebo, to the top of Pisgah that is over against Jericho. The LORD shewed him all the land of Gilead, unto Dan" Deuteronomy 34:1).**

God allowed Moses to view the Promised Land. But God told Moses, **"I have caused thee to see it with thine eyes, but thou shalt not go over thither. So Moses the servant of the LORD died there in the land of Moab, according to the word of the LORD And He (God) buried him in the valley in the land of Moab" (Deuteronomy 34:5 – 6).** Clearly, Moses was one of God's greatest leaders and perhaps God's greatest and most humble human leaders recorded in the Bible. Yet when he crossed the line, as discussed in this book, God forgave him; however, God held him accountable. He received severe consequences – not being permitted to enter or lead the children of Israel to the Promised Land. Furthermore, he died in the land of Moab after God showed him the Promised Land. He was still healthy and full of vitality, and his eyes were not even dim when he died (Deuteronomy 34:4 – 7).

One great attribute of Moses is that he did not shift the blame to others for his behavior. He could have arguably blamed the children of Israel when he threw down and broke the tablets on which God Himself had written the Ten Commandments. But he did not play the blame game. Similarly, he might have blamed the children of Israel – for their lack of patience and ingratitude – causing him to strike the rock instead of speaking to it, but he did not. He took responsibility and held himself accountable.

When God told him that he would not lead the children into the Promised Land, he might have pleaded with God – he had pleaded with God not to destroy the children of Israel in the wilderness – but he did not plead on his own behalf. He accepted responsibility, accountability, and the consequences of whatever he did. So if God executed accountability and consequences tempered with mercy, grace, and forgiveness.

God forgives Moses – His faithful and humble leader; however, He did not permit Moses to enter the Promised Land. Moses was in full vigor and strength when God called him home. The Bible records, **"And**

Moses was a hundred and twenty years old when he died: his eye was not dim, nor his natural not abated" (Deuteronomy 34:7). Evidently, Moses was still physically vigorous and could have led the children of Israel to the Promised Land; however, God chose not to allow him that privilege – as a consequence of a time when he did not glorify God before the children of Israel. Apparently, Moses had completed the assignment given to him, or God modified the assignment as He chose.

Nevertheless, God called Moses home to be with Him and gave Moses a unique honor. God buried the body of Moses Himself. God's grace and mercy are more than amazing! God forgives Moses through His grace and mercy, yet He held him accountable and allowed him to experience 'some' consequences for unaccepted, displeasing behavior – he did not get to the earthly Promised Land.

There are people in our society and world with a distorted view that there is no accountability or consequence for their behavior. We see that even two of God's great leaders – Moses and Aaron – who led the children of Israel out of slavery in Egypt received negative consequences for their unacceptable behavior, even though the gracious and merciful God forgives them for their follies.

Again, I restate and emphasize the point that forgiving someone for some great atrocities does not mean that the person will not be held accountable and experience consequences – albeit with grace and mercy. Forgiveness is key to the Kingdom of God – we forgive others, and God forgives us.

No one who refuses to forgive someone is preparing to enter the Kingdom of God. And no one is above accountability and the consequences thereof.

Moses is a model of someone who accepted accountability for his behavior and whom God forgave and mitigated the consequences of his greatest misdeeds. Perhaps you and I can learn valuable lessons from incidents in the life of Moses as discussed in this book and recorded in greater detail in 'Moses' Books of the Bible: Genesis, Exodus, Leviticus, Numbers, and Deuteronomy – the Pentateuch.

King David

King David is the final Old Testament example of forgiveness with a consequence, which I will include in the conclusion of this book to illustrate that forgiveness, accountability, and consequences are not mutually exclusive.

God appointed David, a shepherd boy, to be the second king of Israel. He succeeded King Saul, the first King of Israel. When God sent Samuel to Jesse's house to anoint one of Jesse's sons to be the king, God did not accept the son who Samuel thought fit the image of a king. When Jesse's last son was hurriedly brought (fetched) to the house from taking care of Jesse's sheep, God told Samuel, **"Arise, anoint him: for this is he" (1 Samuel 16:12).** Samuel anointed David as king. **"And the Spirit of the LORD came upon David from that day forward" (1Samuel 16:13).** The shepherd boy was God's choice to be the king of Israel.

David was a special young man. Samuel described David as a man after God's own heart (1Samuel 13:14). David was a great king who led Israel in successful wars against the enemies of Israel. He loved God sincerely and walked closely with God. However, he was a human being, susceptible to lust and temptation. He was a married man, even married to the daughter of his predecessor, King Saul, and he had at least one other wife.

Well, one evening, King David went on the roof of his house and looked over across Uriah's house and saw Uriah's wife, Bathsheba, bathing. He lusted for the beautiful lady. He usurped his kingship authority and brought the lady to his palace and went to bed with her. She got pregnant. Uriah was one of his soldiers on the battlefield fighting on behalf of David. David arranged for Uriah to be killed in battle by enemy forces. I have discussed this incident at length in a previous section of the book. Following the death of Uriah, David married Bathsheba.

God sent the Prophet Nathan to confront and rebuke David for his egregious sins – lust, envy, covetousness, adultery, and murder. Yet God granted forgiveness to David through his grace and mercy. The Law of Moses required that David be executed (Exodus

21:24). However, David repented, and God spared his life. Nathan told David, **"The LORD also hath put away thy sin; thou shalt not die" (2 Samuel 12:13)**. However, God held David accountable, albeit with grace and mercy, for his extraordinary sins.

Nathan told David (that although he will not die), **"...the child also that is born unto thee shall surely die" (2 Samuel 12:14).** The love- child would not live. Bathsheba gave birth to a child – a boy. He fell ill. David fasted for seven days and prayed that God would heal the boy. But God did not restore health to the child. God would execute a severe consequence on David through the child. David continued to pray and fast on behalf of the child: **"And it came to pass on the seventh day, that the child died" (2 Samuel 12:18).**

David received God's forgiveness, with grave consequences, for the aforementioned despicable sins. God was merciful to man after his own heart and forgave him; however, God held him accountable and meted merciful consequences to him – the death of the child.

It is noteworthy that David promptly repented when Nathan confronted him. And God forgives him immediately – when he repented – from what might have been immediate spiritual and physical death. A remorseful and repentant heart facilitates forgiveness and restoration of fellowship. Again, I want to emphasize that forgiveness does not necessarily exonerate a person from all infractions. God forgives David, but He did not restore the health of that child.

There were other severe consequences that Nathan pronounced on David as well. What he did with Uriah's wife in secret, others would do to his wives in public (2 Samuel 12:11-2). David's own son, Absalom, slept with his concubines (secondary wives) publicly. (See 2 Samuel 16:21 – 22). As a result of God's forgiveness of David, he wrote one of the greatest prayers in the Bible. He asked God, **"Create in me a clean heart, O God; and renew a right spirit within me." (Psalm 51:10).** Please see Psalm 51 for the entire solemn prayer.

As a Christians-believer, you must constantly pray for and practice an attitude of forgiveness. And remember that it might be impossible for you to forgive some atrocities against you of your own volition alone – you need a miracle. Some forgiveness will require praying and fasting. Recall what Jesus told his disciples when they could not cast out the evil spirit out of the young man – 'that some miracles are only possible through praying and fasting.' Well, it will take praying and fasting to forgive and especially to forget some of the evil that is being perpetrated in our community and around the world – unjustifiable wars and destructions, falsehood, scamming, deceptions, and so forth. And yet you and I must forgive if your destination is the Kingdom of God.

Nevertheless, to repeat, forgiving someone is not to nullify accountability and all consequences. Forgiveness might be preceded by accepting responsibility, chastisement, repentance, remorsefulness, apologies, and some level of consequences –mitigated by grace and mercy.

The wise man reminds us that we should not spare the rod (refuse to hold someone accountable and exercise consequence with grace) and spoil the child – should not – aid and abet the child or person in unacceptable behavior (Proverbs 13:24). Individuals, government and society will do well in heeding the admonition of the proverb of the wise man to hold people accountable for their behavior, regardless of their position or status in society.

Forgiveness is the key that opens the Door – Jesus Christ to the Kingdom of God. So be quick to forgive and to seek God's forgiveness (Matthew 6:12, 14 – 15)!

Forgiveness with Consequences: New Testament Example

The Apostle Paul

In this book summary, I briefly discuss a person whom Jesus Christ forgives, with consequences, and who has arguably had and continues to have, perhaps, the greatest impact on the growth and doctrine of the early Church and the Church today, respectively. I speak of no other than Saul of Tarsus.

Saul was a well-educated Jewish man. He left his home in Tarsus – a Roman city and went to Jerusalem to study under the Jewish Rabbi Gamaliel. It is said that Saul had the equivalent of three doctorates in Theology.

By the time Jesus started His Earthly ministry, Paul was a well-recognized authority on Jewish laws. He had the distinction of being a Jew, a Pharisee, and a Roman citizen. When Saul spoke, people listened. Saul was prominently at the stoning of the first recorded martyr – a follower of Jesus – Stephen (Acts 7:57 – 58:1; 22:20). However, in Paul's (Saul's) own confession later, he disclosed to King Agrippa that he had been involved in the killing and punishing followers of Jesus prior to the stoning of Stephen (Acts 26:10 – 11).

Paul then disclosed his conversion to King Agrippa. Paul and his traveling companions were on their way from Jerusalem to Damascus to persecute the followers of Jesus. He recounts his life-changing incident to King Agrippa: **"Whereupon as I went to Damascus with authority and commission from the chief priests (to persecute followers of Jesus" (Acts 26:12).** Paul saw a bright light at midday and was struck to the ground and heard a voice saying, **"Saul, Saul, why persecutes thou me? It is hard to kick against the prick (goad)" (Acts 26:14).** Paul recounted his conversion to King Agrippa and explained to Agrippa that he was being persecuted by Jewish religious because he was now preaching and teaching the Gospel about Jesus (Acts Chapter 26). See

Acts Chapter 9 for the initial incident of Saul's conversion.

Jesus commissioned the disciples Ananias at Damascus to go and minister to Saul. Understandably, Ananias was hesitant at first to follow Jesus' instruction to minister to the persecuting, temporary sightless Saul. However, Jesus told Ananias, **"Go thy way for he is a chosen vessel unto me. To bear my name before the Gentiles, and kings, and the children of Israel: For I will shew him how great things he must suffer for my name's sake" (Acts 9:15 – 16).** Ananias obeyed the exhortation and assurance of Jesus and ministered to Saul.

After three days without sight, the previously devoted and sincere persecutor of followers of Jesus was converted – accepted Jesus as his Savior, regained his physical sight, and received spiritual sight as well. And as they say, 'the rest is history' – Paul (Saul) devoted the rest of his life to telling Jesus' Story.

Jesus forgives Saul (Paul) with significant positive and negative consequences. Paul became, arguably, the greatest evangelist and church planter recorded in the Bible – Old Testament and New Testament. And Paul suffered on behalf of Jesus Christ, perhaps more than any person in the Bible–Job might be an exception. The positive and negative consequences that Jesus pronounced on Saul (Paul) in Acts of the Apostles Chapter 9:15 – 16 were fulfilled during the life of Paul. The writings, preaching, and teaching of Paul continue to impact churches and lives around the world today.

Paul-the converted Saul, testified about Jesus Christ to kings, emperors, jailors, Jews, Gentiles, and to many nations in the known world of his time. He is credited with writing thirteen (13) of the twenty-seven (27) Books-Epistles of the New Testament, and many Bible scholars have given him credit for writing the Book-Epistle of Hebrews, which would give him credit for fifteen (14) Books-Epistles of the New Testament. This writer believes that if the Apostle Paul did not write the Epistle to the Hebrews, Paul's writing, teaching, and preaching certainly influenced the writer or writers of that Epistle.

Yet, with the forgiveness Jesus gives to Paul (Saul) and with all the great doctrines, teachings, and preaching, and the planting and growth of the early churches of Paul, he was not completely exonerated from being accountable for his pre-conversion evil deeds, and he was not completely shielded from all negative consequences. Just to name a few: during his First Missionary Journey, he was stoned at Lystra and left for dead.

During his entire post-conversion life, the Jewish religious leaders sought to kill him because he was preaching and teaching that Jesus Christ of Nazareth is the Son of God and the long awaited-Promised Messiah. He was most hated because of his teaching that salvation is based on the believer's faith through the abundant grace of God and not through trying to keep Jewish laws or by doing good deeds. Paul was particularly despised by Jewish religious leaders because of his teaching that there was no requirement for Gentiles or Jews to have Jewish ceremonial physical circumcision in order to receive salvation. Rather, salvation is a gift of God to those who accept Jesus Christ as Lord and Savior,

Paul, as Jesus had pronounced, was persecuted for the very same message for which he had once persecuted the believers in Jesus-followers of Jesus. Interestingly, years later, Paul wrote to the Galatian churches, **"Be not deceived; God is not mocked: for whatsoever a man soweth, that shall he also reap" (Galatians 6:7).** At the time, Paul wrote to the Galatians – shortly after his First Missionary Journey – his persecution had just begun. He would endure greater persecution and hardship, including a ship wreak on his first journey to Rome for his appeal to the Roman Emperor. He was stung by a poisonous snake on the island of Miletus. He endured house arrest in Rome, where he wrote his prison Epistles: Ephesians, Philippians, Colossians, and Philemon.

Paul suffered 'real' imprisonment in a Roman prison where he was cold and probably ill. He was falsely accused, with other Jews, of burning down Rome. He was a scapegoat. He is believed to have been beheaded at the instruction of the Roman Emperor Nero. So the Bible's great theologian, teacher, preacher, evangelist, church planter (former persecutor), and defender of Christianity-believers of and followers of Jesus, whom Jesus forgave, did great deeds on behalf of Jesus.

Nevertheless, he accepted responsibility for his deeds and misdeeds, and Jesus forgave him, held him accountable, and gave him a great assignment, which he accomplished beyond measure. He spent his converted (born-again) life doing good deeds. He modeled Jesus. '...Paul was filled with the Holy Spirit and went about teaching and preaching the gospel and planting churches (Act 10:38).

We thank Jesus for forgiving Saul and for holding him accountable so that he repented for his transgression; however, faced mitigated-merciful) consequences by God's grace. Perhaps, Jesus is sending the message that no one who is guilty should be totally exonerated without any consequence at all. However, despite the severity of the infractions, Jesus stands ready to forgive – even if it is with some consequences.

The incident of Saul/Paul should strengthen the resolve of Christian-believers to forgive and restore their relationships. In the first place, a burden is removed from the heart of a person who truly forgives. And who knows, the person who receives forgiveness – like Saul may be transformed into a person like the (converted Saul)-Paul. Nevertheless, remember that remorsefulness and repentance are good indicators that a believer is really seeking forgiveness.

Whether you are seeking forgiveness from a human or from God, be sure that you are sincere. You have no control over the sincerity of a person who seeks your forgiveness, so try not to be judgmental. Accept the plea for forgiveness as genuine. The person may deceive you, but he or she cannot deceive God. Jesus reminds us that forgiving is not optional for those who seek God's forgiveness **"For if ye forgive men (others) their trespasses, your heavenly Father will also you" (Matthew 6:14).**

Final Thoughts and Call To Action

If you are a born-again Christian- believer, as Jesus explained to Nicodemus (John 3:3 – 8); or **"You have confessed Jesus with your mouth ad believe in your heart that God hath raised him from the dead, thou shall be saved" (Romans 10:9);** or you have repented, **"Then Peter said unto them, Repent, and be baptized every one of you in the name of Jesus Christ for the remission of sins, and ye shall receive the gift of**

the Holy Ghost/Holy Spirit" (Acts 2:38). [Please note that baptism is the outward expression of the inward confession that you have accepted Jesus Christ as Lord and Savior]. If you meet any of the aforementioned criteria, the Spirit of Jesus is in you, and you have what it takes to forgive, as Jesus teaches and as I have discussed throughout this book. Our emphasis is on forgiving and seeking God's forgiveness in order tp enter the Kingdom of God through the only Door-Jesus Christ.

If you are a not-yet believer and you have devoted your precious time to reading this book thus far, I urgently invite you to become a believer in Jesus Christ and start enjoying the joy of true forgiveness. Please review the criteria for becoming a Christian-believer discussed (previously) above. Then close your eyes, if it is convenient to do so, and ask God to forgive you for any wrong you have done – be specific if you can. Jesus teaches that we should make our request to God in His (Jesus' name). So do that, and accept God's forgiveness. That's all it takes for the not-yet believer to accept Jesus as Savior. Be sincere and remorseful in confessing your sins-wrongs to God, and ask His forgiveness in the name of Jesus.

Jesus has already paid the wages of your sins by dying on Calvary's Cross so that you can have the Gift of God, which is eternal life-salvation (Romans 6:23). Jesus wants you to have eternal life; He has paid for it with His blood. God wants to forgive your sins and grant you the Gift of God-salvation. God gave-sent His only begotten Son (to humanity, as the substitutionary, sacrificial Lamb of God), that whosoever (you and me) believes in Him shall not perish, but have everlasting life-salvation (John 3:16).

Once you have accepted God's forgiveness and Jesus as your Savior, you can seek out a "Christian" church with which you want to worship and have the pastor or bishop baptize you as an outward expression of your inner confession-salvation. Talk with other spiritually mature Christian- believers and reputable-Christlike church leaders for their assistance in your exciting new journey.

Now that you are a Christian, a born-again believer, and the Spirit of Jesus is in you, you are able to grow in your trust-faith in Jesus and 'the miracle of forgiveness. You may stumble and even fall – finding it difficult to forgive at times – but always seek God's help in forgiving others as you seek God's forgiveness for yourself. And pray that others will have forgiving hearts as well!

The Miracle of Forgiveness Might Require Praying and Fasting

Remember that genuine forgiveness – forgiving others – is one of the most difficult things that Jesus has instructed His followers-believers to do. Forgiveness requires love, humility, patience, empathy, caring, and sometimes even sympathy. Some forgiveness will definitely require a miracle which is accomplished through praying and fasting. Jesus told His disciples, **"Howbeit this kind (evil spirit) goeth not out but by prayer and fasting (requires a miracle)" (Matthew 17:21).** The Spirit of Jesus, which is in you, will assist you with the miracle of forgiveness.

Remind yourself of what the great Apostle Paul says. **"I (you and I) can do all things through Christ which strengtheneth me" (Philippians 4:13).** Paul had the Spirit of Christ in him, and so do we. So practice forgiveness, even when it is seemingly impossible to do so. You must forgive because forgiveness is the key to the Door-Jesus into the Kingdom of God. And you need God's forgiveness (Matthew 6:14). So, in the final analysis, you need to forgive others just as much as you need God's forgiveness, and vice versa. So, make deliberate and intentional forgiveness a way of life and ask God to help you to forgive.

You must constantly seek God's forgiveness with sincerity and remorsefulness regularly – use the key to the Door to the Kingdom of God – forgiveness on an ongoing basis. Bear in mind the struggle the great Apostle Paul endured; he puts it this way, **"For the good that I would I do not: but the evil which I would not, that I do" (Romans 7:19).** This confession of Paul reminds us that we are vulnerable to temptation and that we must remain sober and vigilant at all times. The confession from probably the most devoted evangelist ever reminds us of our own vulnerability and our need to stay in a relationship and fellowship with God, always forgiving others and always seeking God's forgiveness.

Chapter 15

Epilogue

If you believe in God and in Jesus, then forgiving others who cause you hurt or pain directly or indirectly is not an option for you. Unless you do not want God to forgive you. Because when you believe in God, you will acknowledge that you have sinned against God – you have disobeyed God in one way or another. When you believe in God, you want God to forgive you of your trespasses against Him; so that you might (will) enter the Kingdom of God through Jesus Christ- the Door. So how do you hold a person accountable and, at the same time, forgive him or her for transgressions against you or against someone else?

As I listened to a professed Christian, who is a high-level government official, proclaim that he would not forgive or forget terrible terrorists for the gregarious attack which slaughtered and injured numerous innocent Americans and American allies in another country, I had a numbing feeling inside. I understood and do understand the need for the leader to appear strong and resolute and the need to project confidence and the pursuit of justice – some would even say, the pursuit of revenge. Then it occurred to me that there might be a misunderstanding of the relationship between forgiving someone and holding the forgiven person accountable. There is no mutual exclusivity between accountability and forgiveness.

In addition, it might have been just being just semantics or hyperbole. I stated previously in this book that forgiveness does not necessarily exonerate a person from the consequences relative to a particular wrong or crime. The Bible is replete with examples of forgiveness with negative consequences. I cited several examples from the Bible as well as from some ordinary – perhaps extraordinary persons. As a practicing Christian-believer, I fully and unwaveringly support, encourage, and urge forgiveness. However, I do not postulate that forgiveness means that perpetrators of heinous infractions should go unpunished – without consequences, especially when there is no acceptance of responsibility, remorse, sorrow, repentance, or apologies. I do not support the tendency of some who aid and abet officials of individuals or even children in wrong doings.

God forgives Adam and Eve for disobeying Him and eating the unbidden fruit. He granted them grace and mercy and even made them coats to cover their nakedness. However, He held them accountable by expelling them from the Garden of Eden but mitigated the severity of the consequences of their unaccepted behavior-rebellion against Him. God could have immediately killed them physically and spiritually – the wages of sin is death. Nevertheless, He forgives them with severe consequences.

God forgives Jacob for plotting with his mother to steal Esau's blessings. God held Jacob and Rebekah accountable. Once Jacob left home for fear that Esau would kill him, he never saw his mother again. But God mitigated the severity of the consequences of Jacob's dubious behavior. Jacob could have died; however, God forgave him with consequences, and the Jewish nation was named after him, and he had descendants as the sand by the seaside.

God forgives David for his adultery with Bathsheba, Uriah's wife, and for arranging for the death of Uriah – murder by the enemies in battle; however, God held David accountable. He did not allow the son of David and Bathsheba to live despite David's pleading with God. However, God mitigated the consequences of David's atrocious behavior – by the Law of Moses, he should have been executed; however, God mitigated the severity of the consequences He imposed on David.

I mentioned that one of the greatest consequences recorded in the Bible, despite mitigation and forgiveness, occurred with God's greatest leader, Moses. God told Moses to speak to the rock that He (God) would provide water so the children of Israel would know that it was God who was providing water for them. Instead of speaking to the rock, Moses, in his frustration with the children of Israel, struck the rock and spoke as though he was bringing forth the water. God forgives Moses for that great error; however, Moses received mitigated consequences; he did not receive instant physical death. However, God did not permit Moses to enter the Promised Land-Canaan, although Moses led the children of Israel toward the Promised Land for forty years.

Jesus Christ forgives Saul (Paul) for persecuting His (Jesus') followers, including aiding and abetting in the death of Stephen and others. Jesus forgave Saul; however, Jesus held Paul (Saul) accountable. He shielded the converted Paul from some consequences, but not all. Paul was persecuted for preaching that Jesus Christ is the Son of God and the Messiah. Eventually, Paul was imprisoned in Rome, initially for the same reason he had persecuted followers of Jesus. Eventually, Paul was imprisoned in a Roman prison and was executed by a Roman Emperor.

I have repeated the foregoing few examples of forgiveness with consequences to make the point that one needs not hold grudges and have an attitude of unforgiveness in order to demand justice with mercy or execute consequences with grace for infractions regardless of the status of the perpetrators. This includes justice for high-level government officials, especially any who are unrepentant and unremorseful.

Political leaders and their supporters must be held accountable for their deliberate misdeeds, regardless of their party affiliations. This does not mean that they should not be forgiven. There is no mutual exclusivity between forgiveness and accountability. In fact, one of the best ways to deal with unrepentant, unremorseful, non-responsive, and arrogant politicians is to forgive them and forget them at the polls – not to reward them for bad behavior. Bearing in mind that God is the ultimate Judge to whom all is accountable.

Similarly, terrorists – domestic or international – must be held accountable, even though believers-Christians might forgive them – spiritual and temporal forgiveness. Holding someone accountable does not mean hating the person. I love my daughter greatly; however, I hold her accountable for her behavior and have chastised her appropriately with tremendous love and compassion – always forgiving.

Sometimes a crime or behavior is so gregarious that punishment – beyond chastisement is necessary; however such punishment must always be done with temperance – not excessively. When there is repentance – an acknowledgment of doing wrong and being remorseful, sorrowful, apologetic, and with sincerity – forgiveness is in order. Again, mercy and forgiveness do not nullify accountability and 'mitigated' consequences – reasonable consequences, always remembering that we, too, are transgressors.

The Bible records how God's special people in Judah disobeyed Him. God sent prophets over and over again to warn them and urge them to turn to God, but they refused. God sent the Prophet Jeremiah to warn Judah's last King, Zedekiah, to return to God and to lead the people of Judah back to God, but he refused. God permitted Nebuchadnezzar, King of Babylon, to capture Judah, severely punish the people, and take the people of Judah as captives into Babylon.

In addition, Nebuchadnezzar killed King Zedekiah's sons before his eyes and then plucked out Zedekiah's eyes and bound him in chains as a common criminal, and took him to prison in Babylon (Jeremiah Chapters 39; 52).

When the people of Judah, in captivity in Babylon, became remorsefully repented and prayed, God forgave them and delivered them from the Babylonian

Captivity through the instrumentality of Cyrus, King of Persia (Ezra 1:1 – 11)

Forgiveness often requires acknowledgment of wrong, apology, remorsefulness, and seeking forgiveness. However, as a Christian- believer, you must be willing to forgive those who are ignorant of the need to seek your forgiveness. This does not, by any way or means, suggest that they should not be held accountable.

There are some people who claim that they have no reason to apologize for any behavior or to seek forgiveness. Such persons might simply be in a state of denial, and the truth might not be in such persons. Forgive them anyway when it is in your purview to so do.

One of the greatest disservices that anyone could do for a leader is to aid and abet that leader in the delusion that he or she has nothing for which he or she needs to apologize. Or for which he or she needs to seek forgiveness. We are observing this type of attitude permeating society today – consider what is happening in the United States and in Ukraine as I write the last few pages of this book. Those who aid and abet leaders in moving in the wrong direction are particularly true for many of those who proclaim to be evangelicals.

Leaders who believe in the Bible will do well to read or re-read the incident in the Bible when Ahab's 400 false prophets (evangelicals) prophesied to him to go to war against Ramothgilead, and he would win the war. Ahab ignored the warning of the one true Prophet, Micaiah, and ended up being killed in that battle (1 Kings 22:1 – 37). Let leaders beware of the source of their advice.

Those who are true believers and are familiar with the teaching of Jesus Christ – who know that they always fall short of God's expectation and have much for which they need to apologize.

Politicians Need Forgiveness Too

I have previously referenced the teachings of Jesus. Jesus taught the disciples that they should seek God's forgiveness, **"And forgive us our debts, as we forgive our debtors" (Matthew 6:12)**. It has already stated in this book that, **"For all have sinned, and come short of the glory of God" (Romans 3:23)**. So evangelicals have a definite moral and ethical responsibility and spiritual accountability to assist our political leaders is understanding that they are not sinless, faultless saints and that they do need to forgive and seek God's forgiveness if they desire to enter the Kingdom of God. It is interesting to note how religious leaders and evangelicals in the United States are quick to proclaim that America is a Christian country or is founded on Christian principles. However, they do not demand Christ-like behaviors from elected officials – regardless of political affiliation and are not holding elected officials accountable for their words and deeds. What kind of evangelicals are we?

In addition, true evangelicals bear responsibility and accountability for doing all they-we can assist our political leaders in understanding that they must forgive others, regardless of heinous crimes or behavior, if they want God's forgiveness. This does not mean exonerating anyone from the consequences of their evil words, deceptions, outright lies, and evil deeds. Jesus teaches, **"For if ye forgive men their trespasses, your heavenly Father will forgive you: But if ye forgive not men their trespasses, neither will your Father forgive your trespasses" (Matthew 6:14 – 15).**

The three key points I am emphasizing here are as follows:

1. Our leaders have made errors; some have made deliberate gregarious infractions against God and man, and some have made unintentional errors and infractions. Some have been hurt by others. They all need to forgive and seek God's forgiveness if they want to enter the kingdom of God through the only Door-Jesus Christ.

2. Those seeking God's forgiveness must first forgive those who have wronged them, or whom they believe have wronged them before seeking God's forgiveness – this applies to those who are already believers.

3. True evangelicals have a moral and spiritual responsibility and accountability in accomplishing the two previous points.

Forgiveness Transcends Emotional and Visceral Reactions

I will never forgive him/them!

It is natural for even a devout believer to express righteous indignation in a hyperbolic manner toward an intentional atrocity that hurts an innocent person. This is probably how America's arguably most beloved First Lady felt when she uttered that she would not forgive the Ex-President for how he tried to defame the citizenship of one of America's most beloved Presidents – Barak Obama. And yet, we know that not every word that is uttered from the lips has been pondered in the heart.

First Lady Michelle Obama is perhaps the most gracious, uplifting, and humble First Lady to adorn the White House – at least in my lifetime. Yet her words borne out of frustration and disgust are stark reminders that others are listening to the words which proceed out of the mouths of those we admire and respect and love. But she will forgive because forgiveness is the key that opens the Door to everlasting life.

Some words are uttered as an emotional reaction to a situation. Even though such words are merely the letting out of frustration, they might be taken out of context and result in consequential negative impacts. Words are powerful, especially coming from the powerful. The truth of the matter is that a person must forgive even the worst atrocity of their perpetrators in order to seek and receive God's forgiveness. Again, forgiving someone does not equate to exoneration and nullification of consequences. So, I plea for forgiveness, even if it is accompanied by appropriate consequences.

No doubt America's 'Former' First Lady, Michelle Obama, has already forgiven Mr. Trump and has forgotten about what he did to her husband. It will be more difficult for some people to forgive and much more difficult to forget the incident. However, that's where the miracle comes in. It will take a miracle. Our First Lady is a spiritual-filled person – a role model for ladies and girls around the world – and is well aware that she must forgive in order to enter the Kingdom of God.

While some may claim that they have no reason to apologize and no reason to seek forgiveness that is certainly not the belief of attitude of one who believes in Jesus, including true evangelicals who embrace the teaching of Jesus of Nazareth.

In this book, I have likened forgiveness as the key which opens the Door [Jesus is the Door (John 10:10)] to the Kingdom of God.

President Biden asserted that he would never forgive the terrorists who committed the heinous crime of slaughtering American patriots and others at the Kabul Airport as Americans and allies were evacuating Afghanistan. The President had every right to be angry and to demand and execute justice – consequences. However, as a believer in Jesus, a devout Catholic, he will forgive in time, and such forgiveness will undoubtedly be accompanied by a demand for accountability and appropriate consequences. But forgiveness is not an option for those who seek to enter the Kingdom of God.

The thesis of this book is that all who want to enter the Kingdom of God must be willing to forgive others and seek God's forgiveness. In addition, I have made the case in this epilogue that true evangelicals have a moral and spiritual obligation to assist political and other leaders and their followers in understanding that those who seek to enter the Kingdom of God must forgive others and seek God's forgiveness. Because all have sinned and fallen short of God's standard, therefore, without God's forgiveness, in no way can you enter the Kingdom of God! In addition, I have made the point repeatedly that those who claim to have a relation with God must demand accountability of their political leaders, similarly to how God demanded accountability of those who led His people – Moses, Aaron, David, Paul, and forth.

As mentioned previously, while I write the final two paragraphs of this book, Russia is invading and bombarding Ukraine, destroying several areas of Ukraine. Thousands of innocent children and women are being killed. How will I tell the Ukrainian Christians that they must forgive the Russians for their atrocities against them? How will we teach forgiveness to those who are perpetrating violent political and human rights crimes in the United States of America? Yet, we must forgive – sometimes with severe consequences.

And yet, as I write, there is breaking news. A lone gunman attacked Robb Elementary School in Uvalde, Texas, on Tuesday, May 24, 2022, and killed nineteen elementary school children, ages ranging from two teachers. The assassin was killed by the police. The eighteen-year-old assassin is dead. He cannot be held accountable. Who should be held accountable, or at least partially accountable, for the atrocious crime against these innocent children? How do I tell the parents, siblings, relatives, and teachers that they must forgive?

How do I tell the spouses and children and loved ones and colleagues of the deceased teachers that they must forgive? And yet they must find the courage, love, and the Spirit of Jesus to forgive. These are challenges for the future. For now, we must ponder the unfortunate situations we see around us and apply forgiveness as best as we can, invoking the Spirit of Jesus to help us.

I pray that regardless of your heartaches, atrocities against you, and your situation, you will seek God's help in forgiving even the seemingly unforgivable. And you will seek God's forgiveness for your infractions purposefully and inadvertently against Him and against others.

I trust that this book will be a blessing to you and to all with whom you share the book or an idea you garnish from the book. I trust that you will strive to live a life of two-way forgiveness – forgiving others and seeking God's forgiveness – using the key to go through Jesus Christ, the Door to enter the Kingdom of God!

Yes, sometimes it is difficult to see how some arrogant individuals will ever forgive or seek forgiveness, but don't be discouraged, and don't give up. You do the praying and leave the miracle to God – some miracles – changes require prayer and fasting (Matthew 17:21. **Remember what the Apostle Paul told his spiritual son, Timothy about his transformation: "And I thank Christ Jesus for our Lord, who has enabled me, for that he counted me faithful, putting me into his ministry. And the grace of our Lord was exceeding abundant with faith and love which is in Christ Jesus" (1 Timothy 1:12, 14)**. Jesus has everything under control. You and I only need to do our part and leave the rest to Jesus. Will you?

Blessings and love as you forgive and receive forgiveness –use the Key to the Door – Jesus Christ to the Kingdom of God!

About The Author

Franklin D. R. Jackson is an American-by-Choice. He earned a Bachelor's Degree from Tuskegee Institute (University) and a Master's Degree and Doctorate from the University at Urbana-Champaign, Illinois. Dr. Jackson earned a Certificate in Evangelism, Mission, and Global Christianity from the Samuel D. Proctor School of Theology at Virginia Union University, Richmond, Virginia.

The author has served in numerous teaching and administrative capacities in a number of universities, including Associate Dean for Cooperative Extension in the College of Agriculture at Virginia State University in Richmond, Virginia; Interim Dean and Research Director for the School of Agriculture, Research, Extension and Agricultural Sciences at Alcorn State University, in Lorman, Mississippi; and Vice President for Institutional Advancement, Planning, and Research at Alcorn State University.

The author has provided consultative services for institutions and agencies in the USA, the Caribbean, and Africa. He is the founder and CEO of Evangelism by Grace International, Inc.

His three previous books are: "When God Says No: Listen for the Yes!"; "Becoming a Joy-Fulfilled Christian in the Twenty-First Century and Beyond," and "Prayers That Move Almighty God to Action." He believes that he has been inspired by God to write 'small' reader-friendly and impactful books.

The author is an active and enthusiastic Bible study and Sunday school teacher. He serves as a mentor to many and speaks at different churches. He is committed to the admonition of Jesus, "Go... and teach..." (Matthew 28:19)

Made in United States
Orlando, FL
30 July 2024